Design Thinking for the Legal Profession

EDITED BY ALEX DAVIES

Commissioning editor
Alex Davies

Published by
Globe Law and Business Ltd
3 Mylor Close
Horsell
Woking
Surrey GU21 4DD
United Kingdom
Tel: +44 20 3745 4770
www.globelawandbusiness.com

ISBN: 978-1-78358-385-0
A catalogue record for this book is available from the British Library

Contents

Executive summary

There has never been a more exciting time to practice law. While artificial intelligence promises to minimize mundane tasks, clients' legal issues are becoming more complex. But, to successfully navigate these changes, legal professionals must better develop and exercise their creative problem-solving skills. For decades, companies in other industries have refined techniques to better understand their customers' needs, uncover insights, and develop new-to-the-world ideas, which are now products and services we use every day. Organizations have concluded that successfully adopting these methods, known as design thinking, can lead to greater financial returns than pursuing more traditional ways of operating.

As the legal industry grapples with increased complexity, accelerated market deadlines, and budget constraints, design thinking holds promise to create a more delightful client experience while also increasing profitability.

The book's opening chapter, by Lann Wasson, associate director of legal project management and Rebecca Holdredge, innovations manager at Husch Blackwell, introduces the fundamentals of design thinking and identifies both challenges and opportunities for including design in the delivery of legal services.

The challenge of introducing such a radically different concept to what lawyers are used to is explored in chapter two, by futurist, John Alber. He argues that if ever there was a discipline ripe for correcting law's ivory tower self-absorption, design thinking is it. Design thinking's human-centered approach to innovation – once the province of professions typically associated with design, such as architects, urban planners, and industrial designers – is now seeing increasing use in businesses of all types, including even a few law firms (and it is being taught in a few law schools). These firms have descended from the ivory tower, and are, John argues, much the better for it.

In chapter three, Meghann Barloewen and Jason Dirkx, Littler Mendelson, look at how design thinking is a user-centered, multi-stage methodology that advocates framing problems amidst deep user empathy and rapid prototyping of creative solutions to service issues or barriers. Their chapter looks at how design thinking can help lawyers better understand their clients' work, overcome their own biases, and define clients' underlying and truest needs. Successful solutions require practiced emotional empathy. This chapter takes a deep-dive into two essential stages of the design thinking methodology: empathizing and defining the root problem. It includes practical experiences and perspectives learned through using design thinking in action.

Design thinking (or service design) is a methodology that has been used in manufacturing and many other industries for decades, but its entry into the commercial legal space has been slow. And yet law is a professional services industry, where success is predicated on client satisfaction. There are many reasons to use design thinking in law firms (and with in-house teams), but perhaps chief amongst these is the importance of re-orienting the practice of law around the needs of the client. The methodology can also be used internally to facilitate widespread culture change, and to instil an innovation mindset within a population of employees who may be set in their ways. Chapter four, by Nicola Shaver, managing director, innovation and knowledge at Paul Hastings, explores the reasons why design thinking can and should be used in law, and provides practical guidance to help newcomers get started.

Design thinking is a well-known methodology for producing work and collaborating in software development. More recently, we have seen other industries adopt design thinking as a way to improve collaboration, increase creativity, and remove bias from work product and process. The legal industry has become increasingly more competitive since the great recession of 2008, leaving firms and departments struggling to find ways to increase productivity, efficiency, recruit and retain talent, as well as deliver excellent customer service that provides a rich experience. By embracing design thinking and the theory behind it, the legal industry – from individual law firms to large government departments and everything in between – can begin to reimagine their workflows and offerings to be in line with current client expectations, moving into 2020 and beyond. In chapter five, Zena Applebaum, director of customer insights and engagement, Thomson Reuters Canada Legal Tax and Accounting, looks at the options.

Legal Lean Sigma® is the unique combination and application of Lean and Six Sigma methodologies, concepts, and tools so they are taught and applied specifically in the context of the legal profession. Legal Lean Sigma Design takes a similar approach. In chapter six, Catherine Alman MacDonagh, CEO and founder of the Legal Lean Sigma Institute LLC, explains how the Institute combined elements of traditional design thinking, then layered in specific Lean Sigma methodologies and tools in order to develop a unique approach to their combined application to the legal field. Legal Lean Sigma® Design is a completely new and distinct approach to improvement and design.

A new kind of awareness is emerging in the legal market. It is coming from both lawyers and business professionals. It is the recognition that new approaches to strategy, growth, and innovation must be found. More and more practice groups and in-house teams are experiencing significant structural, cultural, and financial stress within their organizations. They are struggling to operate their existing business platform while also exploring, testing, and launching new ways of working and new service models. Design thinking is a problem-solving opportunity-finding method that turns traditional business strategy-making on its head. Its popularity within legal has been growing exponentially recently. In chapter seven, Josh Kubicki of Bold Duck Studio argues that clients, firms, inhouse teams, and the entire legal ecosystem stand to gain from this new mindset and methodology, if – and only if – enthusiasm can be accompanied by actual execution. Design itself is not the cure-all, but is a potent tool to add to the leader's arsenal that will better equip them to make real, sustainable, and desirable change happen. It is wonderful that there is a growing design-interested community in legal. It is imperative that this community advances its maturity and capabilities in order to tackle the systemic and cultural challenges that lie ahead.

Every day the legal industry is inundated with announcements about new innovative solutions. From all sides, organizations are pursuing new ways to deliver services, new products and even new business models. Yet, in the rush to adopt technology and appear "innovative", organizations often lose sight of their customers and the needs they aim to solve. As a human-centered approach to innovation, design thinking starts with the customer and includes a number of mindsets and techniques to uncover insights that can lead to ideas, and ultimately solutions, that delight clients. Chapter eight, by Lann Wasson, focuses on the role that empathy, observation, and collaboration play in learning to see problems from different points of view. Examples of various ways to practice building one's creative muscles and real-world examples of how to develop and communicate insights to teams are included.

Tess Blair, of Morgan, Lewis & Bockius LLP, writes about and lectures on legal design and delivers a program called a "Legal Design Jam" that uses elements of human-centered design thinking, six sigma, legal project management and a heaped helping of finesse to leverage what would otherwise be unique constraints in the legal environment (i.e. lawyers) to maximize the potential outcome of a legal design exercise. Tess uses what she calls "psych-ops jujitsu" to turn the challenges in legal (i.e. lawyers) into assets that optimize the time, engagement, and outcomes of their exercises to deliver client-centered solutions. Tess has spent a lot of time observing lawyers in their natural habitat, studying the unique business structure of law firms, and speaking with and following the insightful work of Dr Larry Richard, the leading expert on the psychology of lawyer behavior. This, combined with her background in industrial design, led Tess to create the Legal Design Jam – outlined in chapter nine.

Clients want their lawyers to (1) understand their business, (2) solve the legal or business problem at hand, (3) make their life easier, and (4) be likable. The five stages of design thinking (empathy, problem definition, ideation, prototyping, and testing) are natural steps to foster client intimacy. In chapter ten, Mark Beese, president of Leadership for Lawyers, looks at the expected results from using design thinking to innovate with clients, which include a better understanding of the client, their needs, context, industry and preferences, increased trust and communication about difficult topics, increased awareness of how the legal professional can help the client, and, ultimately, increased client loyalty.

Partnership track, the "T-shaped lawyer," the "Delta Model of Lawyer Competency"... there are models out there that tell you what you should want or how you should build your legal career. But as a law student, young lawyer, or accomplished attorney, what if you still haven't really found "what you want to be when you grow up"? Chapter 11, by Amani Smathers, senior legal solutions architect at Davis Wright Tremaine, and Amy Monaghan, practice innovations manager at Perkins Coie, builds on Bill Burnett and Dave Evans's *Designing Your Life* book to help those in the legal profession use design thinking to design a career that is personally fulfilling.

How great would it be if you could grab 20 people from your office, have them block their calendars for three days, bring in your key clients, and do a full-on design thinking workshop to create the next great firm-client product? Um, really great, actually. (You should try it!) But you work in legal, where that sort of thing is not all that simple to pull off. So, is design thinking off the table?

Luckily, no – argue Andy Peterson and Kate White of Design Build Legal. In chapter 12, they demonstrate how there are practical ways to infuse your daily work with aspects of design thinking. From turning around that group meeting that always devolves into a complaint session; solving a challenge by expanding the number of voices in the room; gaining buy-in from leadership around making new investments; to creating stronger relationships between your firm and your clients.

In the second of his two chapters, Mark Beese discusses how, when teaching design thinking for legal, there are six mindsets that drive innovation. These mindsets are human centered, radical collaboration, show, not just tell, prototype, bias towards action, and trusting the design thinking process. For some legal professionals, however, these mindsets are counter-intuitive and take some time and effort to master. In chapter 13, Mark discusses how to overcome potential lawyers' reluctance, and to master the mindsets.

How do you in reality make service design work in the legal industry and within large global law organizations? In chapter 14, Alex Smith of iManage RAVN delivers practical lessons from the front line of creating a service design approach within an innovation program – outlining how and where service design can make tangible changes to the way legal service is delivered. Alex also looks at how to bring a product approach using user-centric design best practice from the technology industry to legal services and why a product focus can influence more than just #legaltech innovation.

To conclude the book, consultant Duncan Hart offers a word of caution. Today's market for legal services imposes considerable demands on firms to creatively address the way they operate. This includes not only the way they go about securing clients but also the processes they use to how they service clients. Design thinking is not necessarily the best approach for firms to adopt, however.

It highlights close attention to client needs and envisages a strong team-based approach to exploring those needs and the rapid development of experimental "prototypes". This approach, however, must be tempered, particularly in the case of law firms, by a recognition that experimentation cannot often be conducted at what might be a potential cost to the client, let alone the firm's insurers!

Firms need also to be aware of the "cultural" requirements that adopting design thinking demands. This requires careful assessment as to the specific context in which such a process can be appropriately deployed. Many teams within the firm may simply be unsuitable or unable to execute a design strategy in view of any number of dysfunctional elements that beset teams. In short, firms need to carefully assess whether design thinking is an appropriate response and process to the issues they are seeking to address. Chapter 15 looks at the potential pitfalls of design thinking.

About the authors

John Alber serves as futurist for the Institute for Future of Law Practice and for the International Legal Technology Association. He writes, speaks, and consults widely, focusing on finding practical ways to reshape the delivery of legal services to suit a future demanding excellence far beyond substantive legal skills. Prior to his current role, John was a transportation industry CEO. Thereafter, he led Bryan Cave LLP to become one of the most innovative firms in the world, serving as its strategic innovation partner for more than 16 years. While at Bryan Cave, he also served for seven years on the firm's operating group (its management committee). John is an Emeritus fellow of the College of Law Practice Management. He has received a number of awards, both in the legal field and in information technology generally. Among other awards, he received ILTA's first ever Premiership Award, was named American Lawyer Media's first ever "Champion of Technology", was given a Lifetime Achievement Award by Law Technology News and recognized as one of the Top 25 CTOs in the world by Infoworld. In addition, while under his leadership, Bryan Cave received recognition as a *CIO Magazine* "Top 100 Company" and was twice recognized as ILTA's Most Innovative Firm.

Catherine Alman MacDonagh is a former corporate counsel and law firm executive. She teaches and provides training and consulting services in process improvement and project management, strategic planning, marketing, and business development. A Legal Lean Sigma® Black Belt and a certified Six Sigma Green Belt, Catherine is the CEO and a founder of the Legal Lean Sigma Institute. It offers consulting and the first and only process improvement and project management certifications, courses, and workshops designed for the legal profession. Catherine created Legal Lean Sigma® and the award winning Legal WorkOut®.

Zena Applebaum is a competitive intelligence strategist, legal blogger, personal brand advocate, and trying to change the legal industry one design thinking workshop at a time. Having been one of the early pioneers of law firm competitive intelligence nearly 20 years ago, and authoring *Business Intelligence for Law Firms* published in November 2012, Zena shares her passion for the industry as a speaker, writer, and a contributor to blogs, including 3 Geeks and a Law Blog with topics ranging from competitive intelligence to change management, qualitative data analysis and personal branding. In 2015, Zena was inducted as a Fellow of the Council of CI Fellows and has been a sessional instructor at the University of Toronto iSchool, Rutgers University and a guest lecturer at law schools across North America. Zena honed her CI skills as the director of competitive intelligence at Bennett Jones LLP for over a decade prior to taking on her current role as national director, market insights and engagement at Thomson Reuters in Canada. In her role, Zena is responsible for client feedback and intelligence, market insights, and sales enablement.

An attorney in Littler Mendelson's Knowledge Management department, **Meghann Barloewen** collaborates with subject matter experts, practice groups and other firm departments in the creation and management of innovative client services in all areas of labor and employment law. Significant areas of focus include new development and content sustainment of the HR applications for Littler's award-winning joint venture, ComplianceHR. Meghann also leads the development of other technology solutions, including risk analysis and document automation applications, workflow processing tools, and other educational materials. As Knowledge Management counsel, Meghann frequently draws upon her prior experience in advice and counsel work and litigation experience defending employers in a broad range of employment matters.

Mark Beese is president of Leadership for Lawyers, LLC, a consultancy focused on helping lawyers become better leaders and business developers. He provides training, coaching and consultation to firms in the areas of leadership development, business development and innovation with law firms and other professional service firms. His clients range from small, single office firms to global Amlaw 10 firms. Mark is an adjunct faculty at the University of Denver school of law and former adjunct faculty at the Center for Creative Leadership. He focuses on issues of change leadership, team development, influence, cross-generation issues, collaboration, innovation and design thinking. He is a Fellow of the College of Law Practice Management and has been inducted into the Legal Marketing Association Hall of Fame. Mark facilitates design thinking workshops for law firms, legal departments, and professional departments – www.designthinkinglegal.com.

Tess Blair is a litigator and legal entrepreneur who has practiced at the intersection of law, technology, and design for more than two decades. Tess is the founder and leader of Morgan Lewis's eData practice, a data-driven practice that combines great lawyering with technology and design to enhance the delivery of legal services. A practicing litigator, Tess serves as national discovery counsel to some of the world's largest organizations alongside her client's trial counsel, and as a core member of the litigation team, she develops and executes all aspects of the client's discovery strategy as well as optimizes her client's evidence gathering, analysis, and presentation. Tess counsels a host of Fortune 500 companies, conducting risk assessments and guiding her clients as they develop internal information governance policies and controls to address privacy, security, retention, and disposition of information and data. As leader of eData, Tess works with her team, her colleagues, and clients to design and develop tools and techniques to improve the delivery of legal services. The eData team uses process design, automation, UX, product design, application development, machine learning, and augmented intelligence tools to develop technology, process, and service solutions built to meet our clients' needs. Tess lectures regularly on civil procedure, eDiscovery, and data privacy – including cross-border discovery and data minimization – and writes frequently on eDiscovery, information governance, and data privacy for a variety of legal publications. She is the lead author of the eData Deskbook, currently in its third edition. Tess also serves as Special Discovery Master to the Eastern District of Pennsylvania.

Jason Dirkx, knowledge management counsel at Littler Mendelson, focuses on identifying and integrating new knowledge management technologies with the firm's legal work processes. He works with attorneys, practice groups, other knowledge management attorneys and clients in an effort to provide innovative client services in all areas of labor and employment law. Jason has worked for several other law firms, developing and globally deploying legal technologies and services. Prior to law school, he worked as a software engineer, developing military planning and readiness software for US Strategic Command (US STRATCOM) and the Department of Defense.

Duncan Hart practiced as a barrister and solicitor principally in the area of intellectual property for more than 25 years before becoming a managing partner at one of Australia's largest law firms. He opened his own consultancy in 2002 in Melbourne, providing management consulting advice to the legal and allied professions. Duncan's educational background includes Legal (LLB) and Master of Business Administration (MBA) degrees. Duncan has acted as chairman of partners and managing partner for various professional service firms, including three law firms and a patent attorney firm and has also undertaken project management consultancies as in-house counsel. He is a regular traveler to SE Asia and China as well as the Middle East. He is a director of several companies involved in supporting the export of services to those regions and the commercialization of their intellectual property. He has lived and worked in both the US and UK, providing management consulting and legal advice. He is based in Melbourne. He is the author of *The Strategic Law Firm* and *Lean Innovation for Lawyers* and a regular speaker at conferences dealing with leadership, strategy, innovation, and marketing issues.

Rebecca Holdredge is the innovations manager at Husch Blackwell and an experienced data scientist, attorney and Six Sigma Black Belt. Rebecca leads the firm's innovation advisory team and the associates legal innovation team and encourages attorneys to create a culture of innovation, efficiency, and quality by developing best practices and leveraging technology. She also engages with clients and in-house counsel to better understand their needs, develop relationships, and collaborate on innovative and effective solutions. Rebecca is well versed in the approach and techniques of design sprints to encourage more collaborative ideation and experimentation.

Josh Kubicki is co-founder and design principal for Bold Duck Studio. He is a former chief strategy officer for a global law firm, worked in Verizon's general counsel office, and has worked with numerous in-house teams, law firms, start-ups, and leading corporations – designing and launching new business models. At Michigan State University, he was an adjunct faculty member where he developed and taught the industry's first law school curriculum on design thinking.

Amy Monaghan is practice innovations manager at Perkins Coie. As a member of the Knowledge Management team, Amy works side-by-side with practice groups and clients to design, develop, and implement innovative solutions, particularly those involving artificial intelligence, document automation tools, and logical reasoning systems. Amy is responsible for educating the firm and its clients on the availability and capabilities of legal technology and is a frequent speaker on these topics.

Andy Peterson has spent a decade throwing himself into designing better experiences for law firm clients – more transparent, more collaborative, and more efficient, where decision-making is driven by data as much as by gut feeling. One of the original contributors to Davis Wright Tremaine's De Novo effort, Andy is proud of how he and his peers took innovation at that firm from a collection of grassroots projects, to a firm-supported initiative for internal improvement, and finally to a client-focused effort to drive revenue, client loyalty, and brand awareness. Andy thrives on working directly with clients to design technology and staffing initiatives that solve some of their most difficult legal and business challenges.

Nicola Shaver is the managing director of innovation and knowledge at Paul Hastings, LLP. Her interest in design thinking was sparked in 2015 when she participated in one of Margaret Hagan's workshops and witnessed the power of empathy and user-centric design to solve problems in a more meaningful way. Since then, Nicola has introduced design thinking at two major law firms, both as an internal driver of change and as an external tool for improving client service and engagement. Nicola is an IDEO-trained design thinking facilitator, and a 2019 graduate of the Helsinki Brainfactory Legal Design Workshop (in association with the Legal Design Summit). She is also the founder of the Legal Innovation and Design Association (LID), a support and education network for innovation professionals in US law firms with an interest in service design methodologies.

R. Amani Smathers is the senior legal solutions architect at Davis Wright Tremaine. Amani works directly with clients and partners to design solutions to legal business challenges. She specializes in process improvement methods, document automation tools, and developing simple systems to manage workflows and turn data into actionable insights. Her favorite projects are those where she sees her work make a real, positive impact on a team's workloads and outcomes.

Alex Smith is global product lead for iManage RAVN, delivering search, next generation legal data and using AI techniques to extract insight from data used in legal work. He heads up the product team, working closely with customers. Alex previously worked at Reed Smith LLP, leading the firm's Innovation Hub program. He headed up a physical and virtual program of client-centric ideas-generation and rethinking of legal service design. Based in London, he managed activities in the Innovation Hub, Reed Smith's unique space for co-creation with clients using service design and innovation techniques. As a user-centric design practitioner, Alex puts the client at the heart of everything he does. He has two decades of experience interacting with lawyers in law firms and inhouse teams to design new products and technologies, primarily as innovation and new product lead at LexisNexis.

Lann Wasson is the associate director of legal project management at Husch Blackwell LLP and holds certifications in project management (PMP), Lean Six Sigma (Green Belt) and Design Thinking (IDEO). For the past 18 years he has worked closely with client teams, practice groups, and in-house counsel to understand their needs and guide the design and development of new solutions from technology platforms to new products and services to new business models. Lann conducts workshops with internal and external clients in the areas of artificial intelligence, legal project management, and service design. In 2017 and 2018 the ACC recognized two of his client projects as Value Champions.

Kate White is the co-founder of Design Build Legal, a consulting company focused on supporting law firms in applying people, process, and technology to design client-centered legal solutions. She has been working with law firm leaders to launch new practice and industry groups, apply account management principles, gather client feedback and insights, and develop client-centered products and services for over a decade. Kate also works with in-house legal teams to develop outside counsel management programs. Prior to launching Design Build Legal, Kate served as a founding member of Davis Wright Tremaine's innovation initiative, DWT De Novo, through which she worked with clients to identify challenges and develop integrated solutions. She holds a JD from Seattle University School of Law and a BA in Journalism from Seattle University.

Chapter 1:
Introduction to design thinking

By Lann Wasson, associate director of legal project management, and Rebecca Holdredge, innovations manager, Husch Blackwell

As law firms, legal departments and law schools grapple with increased complexity and ambiguity in the marketplace, there is a growing need to exercise a more robust set of creative problem-solving skills. Particularly in a crowded market, the ability to differentiate services on the basis of the customer and client experience has taken center stage. Whether one is considering the application of artificial intelligence, the automation of business processes, the penetration of new market entrants, the growing sophistication of legal operations, or the increased competition between established players, legal professionals are searching for methods to tailor their offerings and capture new business opportunities. Over the past few years a number of these professionals have turned to a design-centric approach, using concepts such as co-creation, rapid iteration and prototyping, to begin innovating on an ongoing basis.

For decades, other industries have refined a set of approaches and techniques, collectively known as design thinking, to understand their customers' needs, uncover new insights and develop new-to-the-world products and services.[1] In essence, this approach is about learning to see through the eyes of one's customer, working collaboratively to come up with as many ideas as possible, and then actually testing the best ideas out with real stakeholders. Before looking at design thinking as originally articulated by the global design agency IDEO and the Design Sprint framework brought to the start-up space by Google Ventures, it's important to understand some of the foundational concepts and mindsets that guide the application of these techniques and the value that design brings to a business setting.

Foundational design concepts

Fundamental to human-centered design is the idea that creativity, as applied in a business setting, can be learned and developed just as one would exercise a muscle in the body.[2] Shifting one's thinking to a growth mindset, finding sources of inspiration and practicing making one's ideas more visual helps exercise creative muscles. Unlike the common misconception that creative breakthroughs are reserved for a few extraordinary individuals like Thomas Edison (whose singular "lightbulb" moment was actually the product of thousands of failures by a large team of scientists), creative problem-solving is considered a team-based sport that requires a high degree of collaboration, experimentation, and practice.[3]

Empathy – the cornerstone of human-centered design – directs professionals to walk a mile, with fresh eyes, in the shoes of their customers. By starting with a beginner's mind, designers gain insights into the way their customer experiences their current situation, while building rapport and buy-in for the delivery of the future product or service.

If empathy is the centerpiece of design thinking, divergence and convergence are foundational to the flow of a project. Throughout a design process teams diverge, by producing as many ideas as possible, and then converge by selecting the ideas that resonate or hold the most potential. While most business professionals are trained to solve problems by generating ideas on their own and running with the first solution that presents itself, or ideally a best practice, design approaches re-frame ideas as questions (How might we…?) that do not have obvious solutions, and then enumerate as many ideas as possible to address each situation. As a result, participants in a design session must become comfortable with ambiguity and take the time to use techniques that enable individuals in teams to build on the ideas of others.

Design methods also embrace a bias towards action. Instead of just talking about a problem, to communicate their ideas participants in a design session make their ideas concrete and tangible by quickly building rough visual representations (sketches, flowcharts, diagrams, storyboards, etc.). By showing "unfinished work", they create opportunities to get early, meaningful feedback. Failure is framed as learning and celebrated since it minimizes the investment of time and capital in ideas that are less desirable, feasible, or viable. Depending on the particular project, one of these three lenses may be emphasized in order to prioritize which ideas move forward into additional ideating or prototyping cycles.

While the techniques to stretch one's creative muscles are available to everyone, it takes time for new mindsets to take hold. One can imagine the difference in sound between handing a score to a new group of musicians versus a quartet that has played music together for many years. Until facilitators and participants gain enough self-assurance, design sessions may initially come across as more theater than substance; but once teams build their creative confidence they can start to use these toolkits to their full potential.

The business value of design

The business value of design is well documented in companies that have taken the time to embed design mindsets and techniques into their organizations. There are a number of companies that have measured the business value of design by identifying the key attributes within an organization, comparing organizations that have a low and high degree of adoption and then measuring the difference in financial or business performance between the two. Starting with the Design Management Institute's reports from 2013, companies such as IDEO (Creative Difference Model),[4] InVision (Design Maturity Model),[5] McKinsey (Business Value of Design)[6] and Forrester (Total Economic Impact Model),[7] have studied thousands of organizations across the globe and reported on their research in the last two years.

This research overwhelmingly suggests that good design practices lead to better product or service quality, greater levels of efficiency, faster speed to market, greater profitability, enhanced market position, greater achievement of business goals, more successful product launches, greater return on investment, and greater revenue and shareholder returns, to name a few. While the methodology, scope, and scale of each study differs, taken as a whole this research demonstrates how established the business value of design is today.

The origins of design thinking

When Tom and David Kelley started the design agency IDEO in San Francisco over 40 years ago, their teams sought to incorporate insights from the social sciences into design. This need prompted David Kelley to start the Hasso Platner Institute of Design at Stanford, now commonly known as the d.school, roughly 30 years ago to allow for students, faculty, and business leaders to work together across disciplines on real projects as they learned the concepts and techniques of design thinking. The Legal Design Lab at Stanford is also part of this effort to teach design to legal professionals. In 2000, ABC featured an IDEO team using these techniques on an episode of *Nightline*, which catapulted the agency and design thinking into the public consciousness as an innovation engine.

Although IDEO is often credited with developing and refining these concepts and techniques, many other designers and agencies have continued to move their work forward. Most notably in 2016, Jake

Knapp and John Zeratsky released their version of the process known as a Design Sprint, following years of testing and refining these techniques at Google and with start-ups while working at Google Ventures. In 2018, after working with Knapp and AJ&Smart – a design agency in Berlin – McKinsey published its own version of these methods called Concept Sprints, formally introducing design as a professional service.

The five phases of design thinking

(1) Empathize

Empathize is the hallmark of design thinking as a human-centered methodology. Curiosity is the core mindset behind empathy. By being curious about our customer's problems, we discover their emotions, stories, and unmet needs. During this phase, team members go out into their customer's world to observe, listen, and reflect on why and how their customers have adapted their behavior in their current situations. Sometimes, a team will focus on extreme users or analogous situations in order to see adaptations more clearly. By deepening one's understanding of the customer as a person, ethnographic research places humans at the center of innovation.

(2) Define

During the Define phase, team members pull together their field observations and package them into informative, inspiring and memorable insights in order to motivate other stakeholders to create better products and services for real customers. Motivate is the central mindset behind defining a problem. In this phase, teams also create a map of the customer journey, as the user experiences a product or service, to help locate the key moments and interactions that will make the most difference in the overall experience. To inspire and motivate stakeholders to pursue bold solutions, teams will often craft stories from their insights.

(3) Ideate

Ideate invites team members to diverge and ask open-ended questions before converging on a few ideas. Being playful is the mindset behind ideating. By stretching beyond one's first thoughts and welcoming ideas that might initially seem silly, teams explore beyond the traditional norms of brainstorming sessions. Ideation is a highly collaborative endeavor and involves team members working alone, then as a group and building off the ideas of others. The focus is on generating as many ideas as possible and often framing the ideas as "How Might We...?" questions in order to see the problem as an opportunity with multiple solutions. Many times individuals will sketch simple drawings during ideation to communicate the essence of their ideas.

(4) Prototype

During Prototype, teams make their ideas tangible and create props to tell the story of an idea. The mindset behind prototyping is "build to think". In this phase, multiple prototypes may be built around one idea to test different aspects of the idea. While many people think about prototypes as physical products, they can also be storyboards, flow-charts, digital role-play sketches (video) or mocking up a space to bring an experience to life. Prototypes in this phase are very rough, low-fidelity creations using readily available materials. Rapid prototyping is also an iterative process as teams incorporate feedback into subsequent concepts.

(5) Test

In Test, teams invite customers to engage with the prototype. The mindset of the test phase is experimentation. Often the design group will observe customer interactions as a team to notice the person's reactions, listen to feedback, and look for patterns from one interview to another. By gathering feedback from real customers, teams fail early and move on to more successful ideas sooner. Building low fidelity concepts also allows teams to test key aspects of the customer experience quickly before becoming attached to one idea, and testing uncovers assumptions in the original idea or concept that might not be visible to those working on the project. Like prototyping, testing is a repetitive process of trial and error as ideas are refined further.

Google Venture's Design Sprints

Since its publication in 2016, Sprint[8] has become one of the most notable frameworks for executing design thinking, first in start-ups and then in larger, more mature organizations. Even at IDEO, designers dog ear the pages of *Sprint* in order to move quickly and let customers guide decision-making, instead of relying on a team's own instincts and opinions. In *Sprint*, Jake Knapp, John Zeratsky, Braden Kowitz and Michael Margolis synthesized their experiences at Google using design concepts and techniques into a five-day sequence of activities during hundreds of consulting projects at Google Ventures. During these engagements the team introduced into the process new forms of structured discussions, story-centered design, time-boxed activities and an overarching focus on key business questions. Over the last few years, professionals in the legal industry have begun to adapt the Sprint framework into an innovation playbook that guides teams that are re-imagining internal operations and client services.

(1) Map

Map involves a team reviewing what is known about a problem, agreeing to a long-term goal, a metric for measuring success, listing the critical questions that address this goal, interviewing experts on the team or in the field, mapping the problem or customer journey, identifying the greatest risks and then selecting a target problem. On the first day individuals work alone and then together as a team using the "How Might We...?" format in structured discussions to generate ideas, group them in themes and then prioritize problem areas. The focus on the first day is to reduce the insights from the team and experts down to that one key moment that would elevate the customer experience to the degree that a new product or service could be brought to market.

(2) Sketch

Sketch involves more ideation, inspiration from design patterns found in existing products, services, or processes and drawing solutions as rough sketches and storyboards. The first half of this phase builds on existing ideas by a time-boxed review of solutions currently on the market. By looking at analogous situations, the team applies insights from the previous day to identify gaps and opportunities that can be addressed by new concepts. The second half of this phase involves a series of activities to sketch possible solutions to the problem, including some individual note taking and practice sketches to reload ideas into one's working memory, a time-boxed series of sketches (Crazy-8s) and a solution sketch or story-board that communicates the central idea. Drawing in a team setting can be quite challenging for professionals who are used to articulating ideas verbally or in narrative formats, so it's important to set expectations, warm up the team and show examples so that these activities are productive.

(3) Decide

Participants initially Decide which solution will best achieve the goal, while keeping competitive ideas alive. They then take the best scenes from the proposed solutions and create a unified story-board to guide prototyping. Teams use a variety of techniques in sprints, such as speed critiques, voting mechanisms, heat maps and straw polls, to guide decision-making toward the most effective ideas. This is the point in time where teams also decide to pursue a single solution or to prototype competing ideas. By the end of the phase the story of the solution takes shape from the opening scene, gaps are filled in, and individual features are layered on using post-it notes.

(4) Prototype

Prototype involves teams building a façade to help customers interact with the key moments of a product or service. Unlike lean start-up methods, teams are not building minimal viable product; rather, they are creating somewhat higher-fidelity concepts that are just good enough to engage customers for early feedback. Oftentimes, mock-ups are used for digital products and spaces, and simulations are used for service experiences, all to accelerate the movement from idea to action. To effectively prototype, teams will often need access to materials or software to mock-up the solution, to divide up and tackle different areas of the solution, then stitch the components together as a unified whole and conduct a dress rehearsal for the next phase.

(5) Test

Test involves conducting a set of interviews to get just enough real customer data to validate the concept behind the prototype. In Design Sprints these feedback sessions begin with one of the team members welcoming the customer, then asking some open-ended contextual questions, introducing the prototype, and asking some follow-up questions based on their reactions. The interviewer must be careful during these sessions to appear curious and not prompt for specific answers or to try to defend a feature or attribute. Often the design team will watch the interviews as they unfold or as a recorded session, and then debrief as a team, so that everyone responds to the same experience. Ideally, five customers are interviewed at the end of a sprint in order to receive enough feedback to identify patterns in their responses. Just as design thinking projects are often iterative in nature, companies frequently incorporate the feedback from the test phases in subsequent sprints to continue to move a product or service toward the ideal product market fit.

Challenges for applying design thinking in a legal context

The legal industry is ripe for innovation, and design thinking techniques could be a key tool in reforming the industry, so why are lawyers slow to embrace it? In many ways, the traditional characteristics of successful attorneys – such as following precedent, working individually, avoiding risk and delivering perfection – are antithetical to the process of design thinking. Most lawyers have never been taught the benefits of sketching to visualize solutions, understanding processes from multiple viewpoints, or sharing ideas even though they may not work. Creative problem-solving has not been embraced or rewarded, so many attorneys have lost their creative confidence. In embracing the design thinking mindset, we've outlined several challenges in applying design thinking in a legal context.

(1) "Who has time for that?"

The biggest challenge may be the billable hour construct within the legal industry. While keeping track of time in six-minute increments only applies to attorneys working at law firms, the mentality that an attorney's time is best spent sitting at a desk doing work permeates throughout the industry. Firms continue to reward attorneys for short-term accomplishments (e.g. the number of hours they bill) rather than quality or creativity. Since this reward system dissuades attorneys from investing time in creative problem-solving or thinking about longer-term strategy, it cannot be surprising that attorneys shy away from activities like design thinking sessions to focus on shorter-term projects.

Even the most open-minded attorneys struggle with the idea of investing a full day working with others brainstorming and participating in post-it note exercises, and cell phones typically divert attention away from the day's topic. Often, attorneys that object to the idea of a design thinking session will try to offer a compromise, such as an hour of traditional brainstorming, not realizing the true benefit of the process. To overcome this challenge, continue educating attorneys on the benefits of design thinking, and since FOMO (fear of missing out) is rampant in today's legal industry, consider emphasizing the wins that others within the industry have had using this process.

(2) Limited viewpoint

The legal industry, in many ways, is often characterized as a siloed profession, prioritizing individual over team results. Being curious about how systems work or the steps involved to accomplish a project has not been a priority. Attorneys often overlook the amount of effort other professionals invest in delivering legal services and, inadvertently, misinterpret the key goals of the client.[9]

Great solutions usually involve a combination of numerous people, teams, and viewpoints. An important aspect of design thinking is ensuring the right people are in the room to begin with (or, at the very least, their input is shared with the team). If only attorneys are asked to solve a problem, they may incorrectly identify the actual challenge or pain point, and any additional time invested in the design thinking process will be wasted. To overcome this challenge, it's imperative to have the voice of all involved parties in the design thinking process.

(3) Imperfection is scary

The legal industry lacks an appreciation for creativity, which is critical to design thinking. Often, individual achievements are valued over group success, which leads to striving for perfectionism while originality and imagination are shunned. Legal memos, contracts, and pleadings are never praised for their creativity, which leads to the "because we've always done it this way" mentality the industry is known for. As an example, one tool often used in design thinking is sketching, as it allows for a quicker and deeper understanding of ideas presented. However, many attorneys balk at this exercise, because sketching is often an imperfect art form and exposes a lack of talent and low creative confidence.

The good news is that creativity is never lost completely; it just needs to be exercised like a muscle that is out of shape. Continuing to find opportunities to be creative will help attorneys rediscover their creative confidence, and incentivizing group wins, instead of individual misses, will encourage people to share their innovative ideas.

While these challenges may be difficult to overcome, lawyers are known to be smart, client-focused, and excellent at issue spotting. Once they can be convinced of the benefits of design thinking and realize they are capable and incentivized to be creative, design thinking may be a tool that is commonly relied on to find creative solutions in the legal industry.

References

1. Tim Brown, *Change By Design*, New York: 2009.
2. Tom Kelley and David Kelly, *Creative Confidence*, London: 2013.
3. Tom Kelley, *The Art of Innovation*, New York: 2001.
4. www.ideo.com/post/creative-difference
5. www.invisionapp.com/design-better/design-maturity-model/
6. www.mckinsey.com/business-functions/mckinsey-design/our-insights/the-business-value-of-design
7. www.forrester.com/report/The+Total+Economic+Impact+Methodology+A+Foundational+Framework+For+Investment+Decisions/-/E-RES42030
8. Jake Knapp, John Zeratsky and Braden Kowitz, *Sprint*, New York: 2016.
9. Safi Bahcall, Loonshots: *How to Nurture the Crazy Ideas That Win Wars, Cure Diseases, and Transform Industries*, New York: 2019.

Chapter 2:
Designing lawyers down from the ivory tower

By John Alber, futurist

I met a senior technology executive once who had recently moved over to legal from a large and very successful consultancy. When asked how law firm life differed from consulting, he said:

"I'll tell you what I don't understand. Lawyers inhabit these lavish office towers and they rarely leave. They make clients come to them. At my old consultancy, we worked at the clients' offices. I didn't even have my own space back at headquarters. I shared."

This observation goes to the heart of a long-time complaint of law firm clients. In annual surveys, GCs and law department lawyers regularly complain that outside firms seldom take the time to learn the details of their clients' businesses. Their advice, while it may be correct, is necessarily abstract and less valuable as a result. This has led law firm consultant Altman Weil to repeatedly urge in its annual recommendations that law firm leaders go *see* clients – that they actually leave their towers and physically visit.

And that's a radical concept.

The term "ivory tower" originated in the Song of Solomon and once meant something of great beauty. But it has come to refer to specialists who are so deeply immersed their fields as to be unable to converse with outsiders. Or perhaps unable to visit them.

And the term ivory tower seems especially apt to characterize the phenomenon our new-to-law technologist observed. Lawyers *do* lock themselves up in towers. They do hold themselves aloof from their clients. Hence the Altman Weil recommendation.

And we shouldn't wonder that lawyers isolate themselves so much that clients complain about it. They are taught an isolating regimen from the first days of law school.

The Professor Charles W. Kingfield character in the classic first year law school film *Paper Chase* captured the quintessence of Socratic teaching in law school:

> *"You teach yourselves the law, but I train your minds. You come in here with a skull full of mush; you leave thinking like a lawyer."*

Kingsfield wielded the Socratic method like a blade, using sarcasm to lead students to the *correct* way of thinking – the lawyer way. And he's far from alone in using the Socratic method that way to terrorize 1Ls. It's part of the fun of teaching law.

Blades come into play in practice as well. Young lawyers are taught that the surgically rendered distinction is the heart of advocacy, the *sine qua non* of effective counselling. Lawyer thinking is drilled and drilled until one day an *expert* emerges, a real lawyer, fit to wage practice on clients without the guidance of the Kingsfields of the profession.

And this gauntlet that each young lawyer runs teaches, above all else, the value of the *correct* – the correct way of thinking, the correct factual distinction, the correct advice, the correct result. It teaches that lawyer thinking, lawyer correctness, is the province of the few. There is law. There are lawyers. And then there is the rest of the world. And it is, to quote Kingsfield, mush.

Nowhere in three years of law school or in the subsequent years of apprenticeship are lawyers taught the necessity of also being helpful. Which leads lawyers to the notion that being correct is also sufficient.

What else can explain the phenomenon so astutely observed by the former consultant? Lawyers are the dispensers of expert advice. People come to us for what we know. We don't need to go to them.

During the 1980s, 1990s and early 2000s, law firm economics were such that lawyers had very little incentive to look beyond their own walls. Margins approached those of Microsoft in its heyday. And there was plenty to do inside the firm – browsing marble samples, selecting artwork. Why go outside? Why learn clients' businesses?

But times have changed. The Great Recession accelerated an already underway shift in the legal services market from a seller's market to one driven by buyers. With their newfound purchasing power, clients began to articulate the need for their lawyers to understand them. Organizations like the Association of Corporate Counsel and the Corporate Legal Operations Consortium formalized and detailed their complaints and created programs to try to incentivize change.

All of which suggests it may be time to come down from our ivory office towers and try, perhaps for the first time in our careers, to think about how best to help our clients in their businesses.

Enter design thinking. If ever there was a discipline ripe for correcting law's ivory tower self-absorption, design thinking is it. A lawyer's first reaction to the mention of this subject is likely to be "Design? You're kidding, right?"

That's because when we speak of design we often attach an article to it, referring to "a" particular design as being beautiful, or elegant. The smooth metallic surface and radiused edges of the iPhone fit that understanding of design. In that sense, design refers to a particular physical aesthetic. And, apart from marble choices, lawyers don't do much with physical aesthetics.

But design is also a process, a methodology used to arrive at a superior end state. And it goes far beyond the physical aesthetics of product creation to encompass the entire user experience associated with a product or service. As attractive as the iPhone's physical design was, the revolution it spawned had much more to do with how users interacted with a wide range of services, from telephony, to email, to music, to photography, to videography.

This process, this way of thinking that is so different from the way in which lawyers typically approach problems, has come to be called "design thinking". It is a human-centered approach to creation that draws from the designer's array of tools to integrate the needs of people, the possibilities of technology, and the requirements for operational success.

Design thinking's human-centered approach to innovation – once the province of professions typically associated with design, such as architects, urban planners, and industrial designers – is now seeing increasing use in businesses of all types, including many of our clients and even a few law firms (and it is being taught in a few law schools). It stands in stark contrast with problem-focused, correct-answer-finding modes of analysis more typically associated with the law.

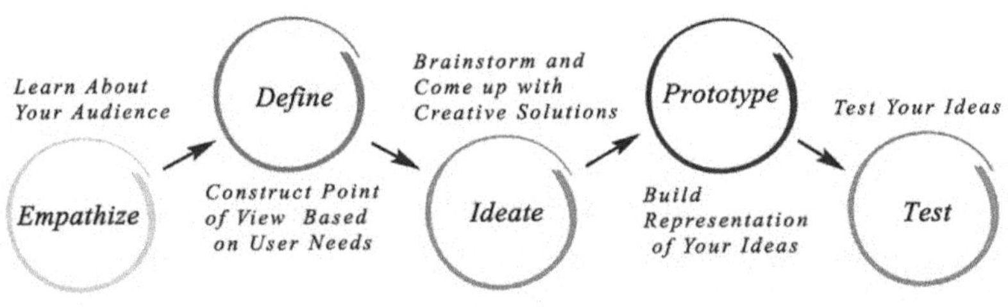

Figure 1: The design thinking process.

At the core of design thinking is something utterly outside the toolset given lawyers in law school – empathy – and is its most important differentiator from traditional business or legal thinking. Empathy goes beyond simply trying to understand a problem. It asks you to put yourself in the shoes of the person who will use your product or service, and to try to understand that person in ways that transcend logic, that draw upon intuition and emotion as well.

Design thinking recognizes the first-level importance of the emotional content of a successful design. When we think of traditional value propositions, we often bring to mind some notion of utility. This product or service will accomplish a certain thing. Lawyers think like that. We will provide you with advice, and it will be correct.

But the most successful designs go beyond mere utility. If you buy a Tesla, the automaker promises that you will receive the safest transportation in the world, that you will be transported in a sumptuous surround, that you will feel pampered, affluent, intelligent. In other words, the design of a Tesla is loaded with emotional content. So too with the iPhone. Its hip exclusivity is as much a part of the design as its elegant user interface. All of the best designs are founded first on human considerations.

And the complaint that Altman Weil and other have fielded all these years – it has just as much emotional content as a "you don't pay enough attention to me" statement in any other human relationship. Our clients have been telling us over and over that they actually want some empathy in our relationships – that being correct is simply no longer enough.

So, how are firms to begin thinking like designers? I hate to say it, because ovine behavior is the antithesis of design thinking. But a good starting point is to begin to look at how those few firms who *do* engage in design thinking are going about it. Notables such as King & Wood Mallesons and Davis Wright Tremaine are well along in redesigning how they deliver legal services, and they're doing it with extraordinary levels of client input. These firms have descended from the ivory tower.

There are also ample opportunities to study design thinking outside the context of the formal design professions. Stanford's Design School runs a bootcamp for aspiring non-professional designers. And our clients, as well as a number of firms, are sending businesspeople, lawyers and staff in droves to learn design thinking.

But perhaps Altman Weil's suggested starting point is best. Leave the office tower. Visit clients. Perhaps even, as our consultant implied, think about living there.

Chapter 3:

Using emotional empathy and design thinking to define user-centered service needs

By Meghann Barloewen and Jason Dirkx, Littler Mendelson

> *"If I had asked people what they wanted, they would have said faster horses."*
>
> Henry Ford (but probably not)

This quote, often used to reinforce the myth of a lone genius knowing what is best for the customer even before the customer knows it themselves, is also actually a great representation of the importance of empathy and problem framing – both key components in design thinking. It is human nature to try and solve tough problems with a "better" version of what you already have (i.e. faster horses), but truly empathizing with the customer's struggle will almost always result in more refined problem framing. For Ford's Model T customers, the more accurate framing of the problem has nothing to do with horses, but something more akin to "I need a faster way to get from A to B…".

Consider an example closer to the legal industry – someone from your organization approaching you with the following statement: "I need to automate an employment agreement". You may immediately start by thinking about which automation tools are available to you, or by finding out if the requesting party already has a template agreement. Now, imagine that instead of starting with the possible solution, you respectfully ask the requesting party why they think they need that particular solution, and you receive the following response: "I need a more efficient tool to draft employment agreements". The user's answer to your simple query may lead you down a slightly different path than you would have gone down had you not asked why. For example, you now may be considering drafting tools or contract analytics software.

Now consider a further possible progression of user statements, each following another inquisitive "why?":

"I need to be more efficient drafting employment agreements."

"My client needs an efficient way to execute employment agreements with executives."

"My client needs an efficient and effective way to protect its confidential information and trade secrets."

Based on simply asking why, you uncover new details, new perspectives, and slightly different angles or levels of fidelity on the same issue. Moreover, as you read each statement your mind likely jumps to different potential solutions. For example, it is possible that instead of a single automated template, you may be better off using a clause library or engaging in some process mapping to help gain drafting efficiencies. These are wildly different solutions than the one originally envisioned.

Problem framing fundamentally affects the way we perceive the goals of the project and the possible solution space. Many of us do not spend nearly enough time and resources to properly understand the fundamental problem at hand and surgically craft a problem statement that faithfully guides the project team toward a solution that maximizes the value for the client. Regardless of your role or project, focusing on problem framing by utilizing the tools of empathy can pay dividends many times over throughout your project.

In this chapter, we focus on the initial stages of design thinking – empathizing with your user in order to correctly frame the problem. This chapter offers some background as to why these pieces are the foundational building blocks of any project and discusses some tools you may find useful that you can start utilizing immediately. We dive into techniques and case studies of problem framing, how to recognize when you need to (re)frame a problem, how to wield tools of empathy to find your way, and how to bring it all back together.

The design thinking tool set

Design thinking is an extremely powerful approach to creative problem-solving. While it originates in traditional product design, design thinking can be utilized in any industry that has difficult problems (also known as "wicked problems"). The methodology is a human centered, collaborative approach to solve tough problems that do not have an easy, obvious solution. In design thinking, there is a bias towards action – plan quickly, test quickly, get feedback quickly, and, most likely, fail quickly, in order to get to the right solution. At the heart of the philosophy is the user – to create meaningful innovation, you must know and care about your user.

Anyone who has worked on projects probably has at least one war story to tell about "the project that went awry" – one that would have benefitted from a fresh take or different approach, such as design thinking, in order to challenge assumptions. However, many of us have been exposed to design thinking via day-long hackathons or as a full-on methodology; most projects and organizations do not lend themselves to employing something this grand, particularly as an experiment. In actuality, design thinking is more of a set of tools oriented around a common philosophy. With this mindset, you can understand what the tools are capable of and deploy them when necessary.

The importance of problem framing

In addition to being open to solutions, there are systemic reasons to why problem framing can be critical to projects. For example, since most lawyers and clients are busy and are not feasibly able to commit to the frequent feedback necessary for something like an agile project approach, many law firm projects default to something akin to a waterfall methodology where requirements are gathered and then the client is not involved until the project is complete. This approach essentially means that you only get one attempt at correctly framing the project.

Another common logistical issue is the enthusiastic client coming to the table with problem and solution already outlined. While enthusiasm and willingness to dig into the details are certainly assets, the client is unlikely to have all of the experience or information to frame the problem or weigh the possible solutions. Simply running with the initial proposed solution could prematurely eliminate a better orientation of the problem and more efficient and effective solutions. In either of these scenarios, framing the problem haphazardly could lead to months of work pursuing solutions that do not effectively solve the right needs.

These types of challenges are unlikely to ever go away – however, some additional work to more deliberately frame the problem from the outset can maximize the likelihood that the end product will align with user needs. A correctly framed problem both captures the hearts and minds of the target audience and focuses your project work in the most efficient direction (ultimately avoiding the impossible task of developing a solution that tries to be all things to all people).

Using design thinking tools, a problem is framed after concerted effort has gone into empathizing with and understanding the user, their needs, and the context in which they operate. Those empathy findings are unpacked and synthesized into compelling needs and insights that will then form the basis of an actionable problem statement. This then serves as a guiding statement throughout the development process and will act to anchor the development to the project's specific user needs.

What is problem framing?

> *"Simple can be harder than complex. You have to work hard to get your thinking clean to make it simple. But it's worth it in the end because once you get there, you can move mountains."*
>
> Steve Jobs

Problem framing at its core is essentially a distillation of your observations as the solution creator, often referred to as a problem statement. It is meant to be a foundational point of focus that serves as a guiding statement throughout your project. In practice, when there is ambiguity or uncertainty in the project, referring back to the problem statement can either help determine direction during the project or identify initial assumptions that may need to be revisited.

The ultimate skill with problem framing is developing something that is a clear, concise, specific, and actionable statement of the problem to solve. The statement should identify the users, needs, and insights on which the project is intending to focus. Ideally, the statement aligns with a deep and concrete understanding of user needs and the problem space.

The need to go deeper

> *"Always design a thing by considering it in its next larger context – a chair in a room, a room in a house, a house in an environment, an environment in a city plan."*
>
> Eliel Saarinen

We all have projects where we have jumped into the solution without first understanding the needs and context. This reaction is understandable because it is much easier and quicker to draw instant conclusions about what we think (read: speculate) to be the correct need/problem. Also, there is often professional pressure to appear to know how to solve problems quickly and easily. It is much harder, but vastly more valuable, to set aside our initial knee-jerk solutions to investigate and challenge our assumptions.

Imagine, for example, a practice group that has asked for a technology solution that it can use to show off the group's substantive knowledge to prospective clients. The practice group leaders come to you with a fully-formed idea and ask for the development of a web portal chock full of article links, sample documents, etc. They are extremely enthusiastic about the idea and about having a "cool tool" developed, but rather than spending some time investigating whether potential clients would find such a web portal, or the resources contained therein, useful, the group is driven by their assumption that this *could* be useful. At the end of the project, significant resources have been invested into a tool that is never used by the group because clients are simply not interested.

In addition to possibly not fully understanding the client need or solution space, our instant reactions often obscure opportunities for deeper understanding. By way of example, we recently interviewed a senior shareholder for a design thinking workshop. At one point during the interview, the shareholder voiced a fondness for the hard copy books that our firm was slowly eliminating. While everyone chuckled a bit at this sentiment (including the shareholder) as sounding a bit antiquated, something stuck about this comment, especially since this shareholder typically embraces many of the firm's progressive initiatives and is supportive of moving our services in new directions. Intrigued, we followed up with another interview to delve into this sentiment further and we discovered that there is an actual deficiency in most of our online research tools. The way the tools are organized prevents users from being able to research the surrounding context of an issue as is so easy to do in a hard copy book. Had we simply been satisfied to laugh off his sentiment as something stereotypical, we would have missed the opportunity to understand some fundamental issues with our current tools and services.

Taking time to empathize

So how do we uncover those user needs and insights to frame the right problem? If you recall the example of the practice group web portal, the practice group leaders were very enthusiastic – but instead of taking the time to determine the most useful resources for the web portal, and whether a web portal was even the right solution for the problem, the team members used their enthusiasm and assumptions as a foundation to jump into building a solution. Everyone on the project team assumed that they should develop this project as it was proposed, instead of looking deeper into the foundational assumptions.

To create truly meaningful innovation, we need to know our clients, care about their experiences, and, as Eliel Saarinen counsels, understand the "next larger" context. As project professionals, it is our responsibility to pinpoint the deeper needs that users or organizations may not totally understand or of which they may not be fully aware. To empathize, we need to challenge all assumptions that are brought to the table, even if done so with great enthusiasm. In design thinking, this is often referred to as the "beginner's mindset" in which you leave your preconceived notions at the door (just as children are wont to do). Before understanding how to approach interviewing potential users with a beginner's mindset, it is important to understand the basic concepts central to empathy.

Understanding empathy

> *"Basic human nature is compassion."*
>
> Dalai Lama

At a rudimentary level, we all understand what empathy is. But there are actually three different layers to empathy – cognitive, emotional, and compassionate.[1] With cognitive empathy, you are able to understand a person's feelings based on the situation. Cognitive empathy can help us communicate with our user since we will better understand the person's drive and potential connection points. With emotional empathy, you are able to feel the same way that a user might. Usually, to achieve emotional empathy, you are able to remember a similar feeling and know how they are feeling. Even if you have not had the same or similar experience to the person, you can utilize emotional empathy so long as you can channel the feeling itself. Finally, compassionate empathy (also known as empathic concern) moves you to take action in the person's best interest. You are better able to suggest how you might go about solving the problem with that person in mind, while recognizing that you may not have found the right solution for every person with the problem.

During a recent workshop with the Littler research services team, we saw multiple levels of empathy naturally emerge. Specifically, one of the interviewees, a junior shareholder, responded to a question about his biggest challenge with a particularly exasperated "I just have way too much work!" During ideation, several groups latched on to this sentiment and suggested wild solutions specifically for him (including just gifting him a month of vacation). When we initially interviewed him, this line seemed like something that may give color to his approach to work and life, but we never expected people to connect with him so viscerally, to the point of crafting ideas particularly to alleviate his stress. We witnessed how truly fundamental and powerful empathy can be, even in a professional setting.

Tools for exercising your empathy muscles

While empathy can be a natural emotion, we can be more deliberate about injecting more empathy into projects. This commitment does not necessarily require large changes. You are likely to find that small changes can make a big difference in your end product. Here are a few suggestions that we have found to be useful:

- Interview as many potential users as possible. If your time or resources are limited, try to reach a diversity of user "types" or perspectives, as opposed to multiple individuals in the same user group. For example, for the research services workshop, we identified attorneys at different levels as well as corporate-side patrons and flex time attorneys;
- When preparing what you are going to ask users during an interview, take care to craft open ended, non-leading questions ahead of time;
- On that same front, let the interview subject do most of the talking during the interview – do not be afraid of silence while they consider your questions. Try to avoid summarizing or completing sentences for them as you might do in normal conversation;
- Keep asking the users "why". For example, if they insist that the solution needs to have specific requirements, ask them "why", even if you may initially agree with them. This pushing will help you get to the heart of why they want that particular solution feature. The Bootcamp Bootleg by Stanford d.school[2] suggests a similar technique called "why-how laddering";
- If possible, immerse yourself in the user's experience. Ask to shadow them during their work;
- If they fail to express their feelings, ask them how a certain experience makes them feel. This question may be a little out of our comfort zone, but it is important to discover the emotions that are guiding current behaviors. For example, when we interviewed patrons for the research services workshop, we asked them questions based on emotions, such as "How do you interact with the research team? How does that make you feel?" or "Tell me about a time the research services team delighted you" or "Tell me about a time you were disappointed with the response of the research services team."
- Here are a few other questions you can ask them that may help:
  - Why did they come to you?
  - What annoys them about this work/process/current solution?

  - What have they investigated so far?
  - What is the business goal and why?
  - What other users are involved? Do they all play the same role? Do they share your frustrations? What are their processes? How are yours the same/different?

Employing empathy to frame your projects

When you interview your users, the most useful information you gather (the stuff that is most likely to drive you to the right, most creative solution) is referred to in design thinking as the "surprising insights". These revelations are the information you would not have garnered on your own had you launched into the project based on your initial assumptions. You know you have had a surprising insight when you have experienced a powerful shift in your perspective. In essence, these "a-ha moments" are you beginning to see the problem and possible solutions in a different light.

More of these surprising insights will likely be captured when you take a collaborative approach. Involving multiple people allows you to look at a user's statement from different angles, which can often uncover new or different interpretations of what the user was actually trying to say. There is a useful collaborative exercise in Stanford d.school's Bootcamp Bootleg called Surprise-To-Insight Leap that can help facilitate that process. As described in the Bootleg:

> *"Place a few surprising observations from your empathy work on the left hand side of the board. Pick one to start and ask your team to interpret the behavior by finishing the sentence, "I wonder if this means that the user ______". Everyone writes down their interpretation, then reads aloud (one by one), and places it on the right hand side of the board, across from the surprise. If an interpretation sparks new ideas from the team, feel free to craft more interpretations and add them to the board. Continue the same process with the rest of your surprising observations."*

Using empathy to frame problems

There are many ways to approach distilling your observations – about users, needs and insights about their context – into a problem statement. A common tool in design thinking is to work on crafting a point of view (PoV) statement in the form of:

[PERSON] needs to [USER'S NEED] because [SURPRISING INSIGHT].

If you have a more complicated solution space with multiple users and needs you can identify all of them in a table and use that to create a unifying PoV:

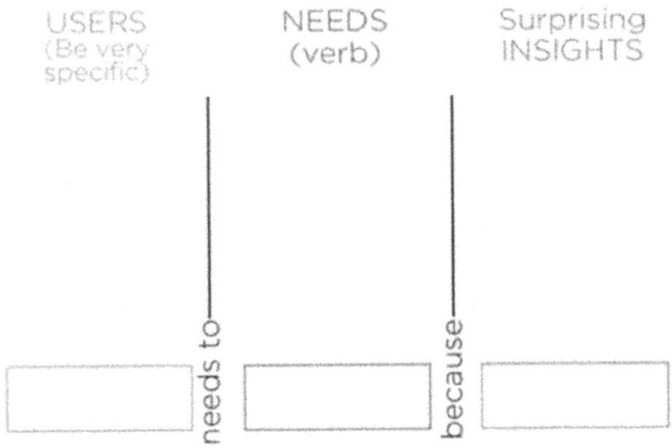

Although much finer detailed (because of the methodology), user stories (from agile and scrum methodologies) are another way to frame the problem.[3] At Littler, we have utilized a slightly different version of these tools by using a combination of a "vision statement" as the overarching problem statement along with more detailed personas and use cases.[4]

Regardless of the tool you choose, it is critical to understand two key aspects of problem framing. First, the process of problem framing in this manner forces you to consider the problem from a user perspective by defining the statement in their terms. Second, a well-crafted problem statement delicately balances specificity and breadth. It is specific enough to focus project efforts in a particular direction (and eschew others) but it is broad enough to keep the solution space open to innovative solutions.

Conclusion

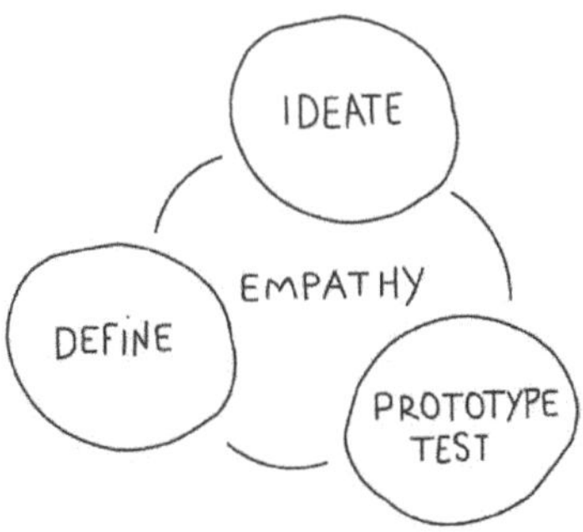

Source: Ines Oliveira – https://blog.prototypr.io/what-blocks-our-empathy-in-the-design-thinking-process-a09766198308.

Regardless of the project, implementing some of these small changes can make a big difference in your project outcomes. After you have empathized and feel like you have a good idea of the problem, you can continue along your current project development process. Another option is to consider dipping back into the design thinking toolbox throughout your process – for example, engage in some brainstorming/ideation exercises or do some low fidelity prototyping and testing with your users. No matter what you do, however, continue to utilize empathy throughout your projects. If empathy is your focus, you can gain invaluable user insights in almost all aspects of project development (e.g. usability testing, prototyping for empathy, etc.) All projects can benefit from making sure you are solving the right problem by deliberately employing a bit more empathy.

References

1. www.inc.com/justin-bariso/there-are-actually-3-types-of-empathy-heres-how-they-differ-and-how-you-can-develop-them-all.html).
2. https://dschool.stanford.edu/resources/design-thinking-bootleg
3. www.jamesshore.com/Agile-Book/stories.html
4. www.interaction-design.org/literature/article/personas-why-and-how-you-should-use-them

Chapter 4:
How and why to introduce design thinking in your law firm

By Nicola Shaver, managing director, innovation and knowledge, Paul Hastings LLP

Design has been used for decades to solve problems in industries outside of law, and has been redefined numerous times in different regions across the world, from cooperative design to participatory design to service design[1]. User-centered design was formally coined by Don Norman in 1986,[2] with the term human-centered design gaining prominence in the 1990s. Design thinking as a methodology has developed alongside service design and other human-centered design theories, but California-based design agency IDEO has been widely credited with popularizing the process. Given the long history and broad applicability of design, it's surprising that many people still think of it as primarily related to product. In fact, the design of services (as well as products) has become commonplace as the science, or methodology, of design thinking has evolved.

Many of the high-profile and successful companies we engage with regularly have used design thinking to develop not just products, but also processes and customer experiences. In our modern world, virtually all of the commercial processes we engage with as customers and consumers have been touched in some way by design. Consider the experience of ordering coffee in a Starbucks, for example, or the technology powering new ordering systems in McDonalds stores, the steps involved in setting up an account in a bank, or the process of ordering a retail item online. In each of these instances, the roles of people, the place of technology, the customer experience as a whole has been considered and designed down to the smallest detail – it's why the experience of being in a global chain restaurant is familiar, regardless of whether you are in London or Sydney or New York.

The use of design to enhance processes or services in law, however, is still relatively new. The five stages of design thinking – empathizing with the end user, defining the problem (and spending time to properly understand it from the user's perspective instead of jumping straight in to solve it), ideating, prototyping and testing (then iterating and enhancing based on user feedback) – do not, on the face of it, fit easily into the practice of law. In particular, the time spent up front on empathy and exploring the problem do not sit well in the fast-paced environment of commercial law, where the focus lies instead on quickly finding a solution.

So why is design thinking useful in legal practice? More specifically, why should you consider using design thinking in your firm, or corporate legal department? And, once you've decided that it is something you would like to do, how do you develop a business case for something that still seems ephemeral and vague to your leadership team? How do you take the necessary steps towards implementing design thinking as a methodology in your legal organization? Where do you even start?

This chapter provides some of the key reasons why design thinking should be considered an essential instrument in modern legal service delivery. It will suggest the rubric for a business case. It will also provide some practical tips on how to get started with design thinking in your law firm or corporate legal department.

Why design thinking?

Improve client service

Empathy

Empathy is core to the design thinking methodology. One of the key features that distinguishes design thinking from other problem-solving frameworks is its focus on the user. Design thinking is "human-centered", and commercial law – in its core application – is focused on corporations. Perhaps that's why it does not come naturally to most lawyers in a commercial setting when you ask them to truly empathize with their clients. In a design session, this is inevitably the stage at which they will start fidgeting, looking at their phones, and searching for an exit. The focus on empathy (and the commercial lawyer's antipathy for the word) also goes some way towards explaining why design thinking has gained so much traction in the access-to-justice sphere in law, as compared to the corporate sphere. "Empathy", if it is considered a skill at all, is often squarely regarded as a soft skill – and thus unpalatable to commercially-minded lawyers.

And yet, law is quintessentially a client service business. In order to excel at client service, lawyers should be regularly considering their client's needs, understanding their clients' businesses, and alleviating their clients' stresses. In short, they should be empathizing with their clients. Indeed, I would go further and suggest that if they are not empathizing with their clients, they are not doing their jobs right.

The departure from an empathetic model of law is something that we appear to have lost gradually, over time. As we have moved towards larger global law firms servicing equally global clients in cross-border, multi-party deals, we have lost touch with the part of a lawyer's role that was fundamentally a requirement to deeply understand the client. Many firms seem so caught up with projecting a particular image (consider the ubiquity of flashy lobbies, spectacular views, slick conference rooms, gleaming espresso machines, and marble floors) that they have lost sight of what really matters. Time and money have long been diverted to things that don't particularly matter, and the wake-up call has come in the form of clients demanding more from their lawyers. RFPs and conversations with clients now make it clear that many commercial entities are increasingly looking to their law firms to partner with them. Clients are seeking strategic partnerships, collaboration, innovation alliances, and services beyond mere legal. Design thinking is one way to start moving the dial back towards true client service.

Listening

On the law firm side, there is a kind of fear around asking clients questions that go too far beyond the periphery of a particular case. For many firms, there appears to be a view that if they have to ask the client something it reveals a weakness, or suggests a lack of expertise. If we have to ask, doesn't it mean we are not good enough at what we do? The irony, of course, is that upon asking clients what they want, a common refrain these days is that they want their firms to listen to them, in order to better understand their business. They want their firms to hear what they have to say before approaching them with a solution. Even better – they want firms to collaborate with them in finding a solution, and they understand that kind of collaboration functions more effectively when it involves both legal and non-legal professionals.

Design thinking teaches people to listen. This sounds like a skill that is innate, and it should be. But it's extraordinary how many people fail to listen when other people speak. Design thinking requires participants to actually speak to users, and, in doing so, to employ open-ended questions. The explicitly stated aim from this discovery phase is to develop true understanding, to appreciate the users' feelings and needs. There can be no question that endeavoring to truly listen to clients will improve a firm's service offering across the board.

Create better lawyers

Lawyers who know how to listen make better lawyers. Similarly, lawyers who carefully consider the problem to be solved before jumping in to match a solution to it will ultimately develop answers and advice that are more considered. Design thinking teaches both of those skills.

Various law schools across the United States now incorporate programming that includes training on innovation methodologies such as design thinking. An example is Vanderbilt Law School's Program on Law and Innovation, which includes a course on legal problem-solving.[3] In traditional law school courses, students are taught to spot issues and solve problems through analysis and application of the law. Rarely are students taught to examine the problem from all sides and consider that there may be multiple ways of solving it. And yet it is precisely this kind of creativity around problem-solving that can turn a mediocre lawyer into a great one.

Along with negotiation skills, advocacy skills, and drafting skills, we should be teaching our future lawyers how to evaluate a problem to understand its nuances. We should be encouraging creativity and innovation in the practice of law, and embracing the notion of ideating and testing solutions. Doing so will improve the legal skills of your lawyers, but it will also prepare them to embrace the changes in process, technology, and the business of law that they will inevitably encounter over the course of their careers.

Further your innovation initiative

Building an innovation culture in a law firm involves a widespread change in mindset. By "innovation mindset", I mean a culture that is open to innovation and creativity in both the practice and the business of law. Driving adoption of new technology tools or new processes, encouraging lawyers to think differently about pricing their work, moving towards productization, developing new business models that will accommodate multiple revenue streams – all of these necessary shifts towards future-proofing the practice of law involve large-scale change. The end-game is to create an environment where lawyers at all levels are open to new things, and motivated to drive positive change.

How do you effect this kind of cultural shift? By necessity, it will occur slowly, gradually. But through design thinking, you can move the dial a little faster. Unlike other problem-solving and change methodologies, which are driven uphill only with Sisyphean effort, design thinking involves your lawyers in the process of change. A design thinking session puts the onus on the participants themselves not only to generate ideas, but also to develop an actual solution to a problem. A session requires that participants delve deeply into a problem and understand it, which makes it an artful educational tool. As long as you implement at least one idea from each design thinking session you hold, the lawyers you work with will see that their own thought process is having a genuine impact. As you work to drive adoption of the solution that is the product of a session, the lawyers who were participants will become your change agents. They will get behind the solutions you're introducing because they have been a part of generating those ideas, and may indeed have suggested them. Design thinking not only taps into the brains of the many brilliant people you have at your firm; change to it also moves the impetus and responsibility for change from a single department to the firm as a whole.

Get things done

Design thinking, in the end, is a problem-solving methodology. The most common method of problem-solving in law firms is brainstorming, which, in corporate settings, mostly happens during a meeting. The outcome of a brainstorm is an idea, leaving the solution still to be developed. Most of the time, the prototyping of that solution will involve many further meetings, interspersed by individual work that is done by various people in a disparate manner. Perhaps all of this activity is corralled by a project manager. It might be weeks or even months before a viable solution is considered developed enough to put in front of users.

In contrast, the outcome of a design thinking session is an actual solution – not just the idea for a solution, but a solution that has been developed and prototyped on the spot. Even if it is a mere storyboard of a process, the solution is one that has been sufficiently refined that it can be taken from the session, and tested with groups of actual users.

This is not to say that design thinking is a shortcut. Instead, it is an iterative process, meaning that the prototype is tested with users and then tweaked and developed, and tested with users again. Depending on the complexity of the problem, the full process can take time, just as in the brainstorming example provided above. However, there are several clear advantages to the design thinking process. First, there is no risk with design thinking that the ultimate solution is one that doesn't actually solve the problem that was expressed at the outset. In brainstorming, because participants jump straight into solutions rather than first exploring the problem, there is a real risk that weeks of work may have to be discarded because upon testing with users it emerges that the problem was inadequately understood. Second, because design thinking encourages rapid iteration and testing, it will be evident to your users well before launch that you are working towards a solution that really works for them. Third, the user-centric focus of design thinking means that you will not be "innovating in a vacuum" – you will be innovating alongside the end-users of the solution every step of the way. This is not just a means towards a truly viable solution to a problem, it is also an effective way to build credibility within your firm, or with your clients.

Improve the bottom line

Numerous metrics have been employed across industries to measure the success of designed products and services. Overwhelmingly, it is now clear that design improves profitability. Design adds enormous strategic value to organizations, with design-led companies far outperforming other companies.[4]

For most innovation initiatives, it's difficult to calculate a dollar value ROI, and this is no different. However, for a relatively low initial investment, it is possible to introduce design thinking into your firm or corporate legal environment and quickly start to show value. If other industries are anything to go by (and I don't know why they wouldn't be), legal services that have been designed with the user in mind will ultimately attract (and retain) clients more effectively, and will therefore drive greater profitability than legal services that have not. Roger Martin, former dean of the Rotman School of Management in Toronto and author of *The Design of Business*, is quoted as saying:

> *"Design-thinking firms stand apart in their willingness to engage in the task of continuously redesigning their business… to create advances in both innovation and efficiency – the combination that produces the most powerful competitive edge."*[5]

We are already seeing success from new-model law firms that have been established with design thinking at their core (see, for instance, Hive legal[6] in Australia). Clients are asking for more from their law firms, and design thinking will help to provide it. In the end, it is the firms that are most responsive to client needs that will succeed beyond their competitors.

How to kickstart your design thinking initiative

Skill up

Before introducing design thinking to your law firm or corporate legal department, you will need to make sure that you have the right skills to execute the initiative. There are two ways to do this – either get some training yourself (and have members of your team trained up), or hire someone (on a consultant basis, or as a permanent member of your team) who has real experience with service design.

In my experience, this kind of an initiative works best if you do both. In order to sell design thinking internally, you will have to know something about it. You may have to demonstrate its value with small groups of people before you get budget approval for an external resource. It's worth getting some training, and attending some workshops, to ensure that the relevant people on your team understand enough to be able to communicate effectively about design thinking. There are some courses (including an excellent series by IDEO[7]) that can be undertaken online. These provide enough insight into the principles of design thinking to enable you to start using parts of the methodology informally – for example, by introducing ideation exercises into meetings, or running diverge-converge practices with your team. However, in-person training through workshops is essential if you intend to facilitate sessions yourself.

When it's time to run a session with decision-makers at your firm, I recommend hiring a consultant. Having an external facilitator will add the necessary professionalism and expertise to your program. Finally, when your initiative gains real momentum, consider hiring a service designer from outside of the legal industry to join your team. Remember that design, like law, is a profession that involves a significant amount of training and education. Just as we would not expect a designer who has taken an online course in law to start providing legal advice to our firms' clients, so we should not expect our lawyers or knowledge management professionals to run a fully-fledged design program without proper certification.

Start slowly

The most concrete success you will ultimately derive from design thinking at your firm comes from utilizing the methodology to effectively collaborate with clients. However, there is also significant benefit to be gained from using it internally. There is no need to immediately kick off this initiative with clients – or even with the practicing lawyers at your firm. Indeed, starting slowly behind the scenes may get you the quick wins that you need to generate the buy-in necessary to move towards external sessions.

In any firm, there are countless problems on the business side of law that could benefit enormously from user-centered design practices. In two different firms, I have had success by starting slowly and using design thinking first within my own department. This approach has value not only because it teaches your own staff about design thinking, and gradually builds support for it, but also because it can provide an early success story on the business side.

Decide on the participant group

Your own team makes an obvious starting point, and starting here will explain to colleagues what the practice involves and why it's useful. Alternatively, start with one business department, or perhaps two who work closely together. Once you have a quick success under your belt, broaden the initiative and expand to multiple departments on the business or administrative side. There are many problems in any firm or organization that affect all departments.

Next move to your lawyers. You can bring lawyers from across practice groups to solve a problem from different angles (this diversity will enhance the ideation process, and has the added benefit of building relationships at the firm). Alternatively, work with one practice group to solve a targeted problem.

Once you have momentum with timekeepers, use your lawyer champions to approach clients and offer design thinking as a service, whether this starts as a listening session, or a workshop, or you jump straight into problem-solving alongside the client.

Note that as you are introducing your initiative, it may also be useful to begin each session with a brief presentation about design thinking. Although design thinking is about doing, rather than talking, part of what you are doing when building your program is educating your colleagues. Presentations are so ubiquitous in commercial settings that you will lull them into their comfort zone this way, before you shake them right out of it.

Focus on the right problem

No one will want to come along to your session unless it is addressing a problem that resonates with them. For this reason, and because you want the session to be genuinely helpful, it makes sense to spend time at the outset to develop the right problem statement to draw participants.

Of course, the ideal scenario is that you are holding a design session because there is a burning issue that must be addressed, and everyone has agreed that design thinking is the best way to do that. For example, a client has asked your team to collaborate with them in solving a particular problem, and you are running a session with that client (with the relationship partner's blessing) in order to develop a solution.

Before you get to that point, however, it's likely that you will need to develop some quick wins internally at the firm, using different participant groups. In these circumstances, there may not necessarily be one obvious problem to solve – indeed, there may be many, and your job (or that of your team) is to identify the one that will work best to engage participants, that will also give rise to useful solutions.

Develop a problem statement

The problem that is at the core of a traditional design thinking session will generally be phrased as a "how to…" statement. Remember that the problem will be further explored, narrowed, and defined by participants within the session – so all you need is a topic and a starting point for the statement. Here are some ideas for problem statements that you may wish to use with different participant groups:

- How to communicate better or collaborate across departments;
- How to improve the project intake system, the business planning process, or reporting to the partnership for administrative departments at the firm;
- How to reduce email traffic;
- How to improve the capture of data around the firm's matters;
- How to better collect/access the information we have about our clients;
- How to onboard our clients more effectively;
- How to ensure we understand our clients' business;
- How to improve the training of our incoming associates; and
- How to break down silos.

When it comes time to work with clients, think about using design thinking to explore your firm's touchpoints with them. What are the processes in place for delivering legal work to the client, and how could those be improved? Ask clients what they are interested in improving around the service delivery model, and use this as the basis for an initial session.

Don't underestimate your lawyers

There is such trepidation around introducing this type of methodology to lawyers. Many of you are likely reading this thinking that your lawyers (and your clients) will be uninterested in design thinking, or that they will scoff at the very notion of it.

At the firms where I have worked to introduce design thinking, the same trepidation and reluctance initially existed. Yet at these same firms, the lawyers quickly became fans and, at one firm, the managing partner ultimately became the biggest proponent of the methodology. Sometimes we forget, perhaps because the discourse around the "lawyer-personality" is now so entrenched, that the practice of law involves creative analysis. Without question, many lawyers will be uncomfortable in initial sessions when there is overt discussion of empathy, or if they are asked to draw instead of write. However, in my experience it does not take long before these inhibitions are overcome in favor of the natural curiosity that lies at the core of these intellectual professionals. Certainly by the time ideation begins, most lawyers will have thrown themselves into the process. Don't let stereotypes put you off launching a design thinking initiative.

Develop buy-in

With all change projects, you need to generate top-down support as well as bottom-up interest to truly gain ground. Design thinking is no different. In order to drive such a program forward, you will need to gradually build momentum through gaining supporters across your firm or organization.

One way to do this is to invite key people, the decision-makers at your firm, to attend sessions. Ensure that you have some practice with the methodology before you do this, so that you can talk intelligently about it, and choose a problem that will resonate with the key influencers in attendance – perhaps even a problem that you know is of particular interest to them. If possible, populate part of the room with people who have previously participated in sessions and are enthusiastic. This is the right session for an external consultant – bringing in an expert will build your credibility at this stage. Make sure you follow up with your key attendees afterwards and involve them in the follow-up with other participants. Once they see the engagement of the people in the room, and the ideas that have come out of the session, they are likely to come on side. If you are able to tie client narratives into the experience, for example by referencing real RFP requests that could be answered if your firm was undertaking design thinking exercises with clients, your rate of success will skyrocket.

Deliver actual value

There is no point in running design thinking sessions at your law firm or in your legal department unless there is an actual outcome from them. As discussed, one of the unique attributes of design thinking is its ability to deliver a result at the end of a session in the form of a prototype that is able to be used and tested.

It may sound obvious, but at the end of a design thinking session you should collect the prototypes and work to implement at least one of these. At the end of any such session, there will be much paper left behind. Gathering it all up and collating a list of the key themes that have emerged over the course of the session will be useful. Get back quickly to participants, to remind them of the outcomes they developed, and include them in the decision-making process about which of these to move forwards, and how. The last thing you want is for the session to stand alone in people's minds as an isolated instance of attempted innovation that resulted in nothing.

Once your program is client-facing, design thinking sessions can provide an avenue for experimenting within the existing service delivery model with clients. Before actually changing anything, these sessions provide a forum within which both client-side and law firm-side participants can come together and think about how to improve the ways in which they interact, the services the firm provides, and the value the firm can bring to the client.

In contrast to the endless meetings that often define our days in corporate legal environments, it is a practice that can actually serve to get things done, to effect real change, and to properly collaborate across departments, practice groups, and with clients. Like anything of value, it will take some hard work and determination to get a design thinking initiative off the ground. However, it's worth persevering.

References

1. https://designthinking.ideo.com/history
2. Norman, D. and Stephen, D. (eds), (1986) *User Centered System Design*. New Jersey: Lawrence Erlbaum Associates, Inc.
3. https://law.vanderbilt.edu/academics/academic-programs/law-and-innovation/
4. www.dmi.org/page/DesignValue
5. Martin, R. (2009) *The Design of Business*. Boston: Harvard Business School Press.
6. https://hivelegal.com.au
7. www.ideou.com

Chapter 5:
Design thinking – a legal industry imperative

By Zena Applebaum, director customer insights and engagement, Thomson Reuters Canada Legal Tax and Accounting

> *"Design thinking firms stand apart in their willingness to engage in the task of continuously redesigning their business... to create advances in both innovation and efficiency – the combination that produces the most powerful competitive edge."*
>
> Roger Martin, author of the *Design of Business*

Over the course of the last decade or so, the legal industry has undergone significant change. From weathering the financial crisis of 2008, which saw buying power shift from the seller to buyer of legal services, to the influx of more than 1,000[1] purpose-built legal technology tools to "help" firms and departments increase their efficiency to deal with new competitive realities, to welcoming a new generation of lawyers who share a very different approach to ways of working, work/life balance, and defining meaningful work than previous generations.

This new reality, with its technology and customer-centric informed rules of engagement, has left the industry looking for new ways to approach customer service, maximize efficiency, recruit and retain talent, and reassess the way it does business. This is no small feat for an industry that has been operating within a very conservative, eat-what-you-kill, hourly billing model for hundreds of years with a long-held belief that its intellectual rigour was immune from the effects of fleeting or modern trends.

Those days, like the days of billing clients whatever you want for your services, are long over. Instead, law firms and legal departments are forced to find new ways of working. Design thinking – a well-known methodology of collaboration and work production native to software development – is being adopted by the legal industry to help define problems, refine processes and enlighten participants on what it can do differently to meet challenges of the new reality and compete in a changing market.

Design thinking – a new way to solve problems

Lawyers solve problems. In fact, sometimes lawyers are hired to draft contracts so that they don't have to solve problems later. The legal business is a problem-solving and problem mitigation business and yet it continues to be plagued by inefficient processes, outdated modes of getting things done, and resistance to change.

Design thinking is an iterative process (see Figure 1) that begins with empathy for the end user in defining a problem before moving on to finding all the solutions in the world without any limitations.

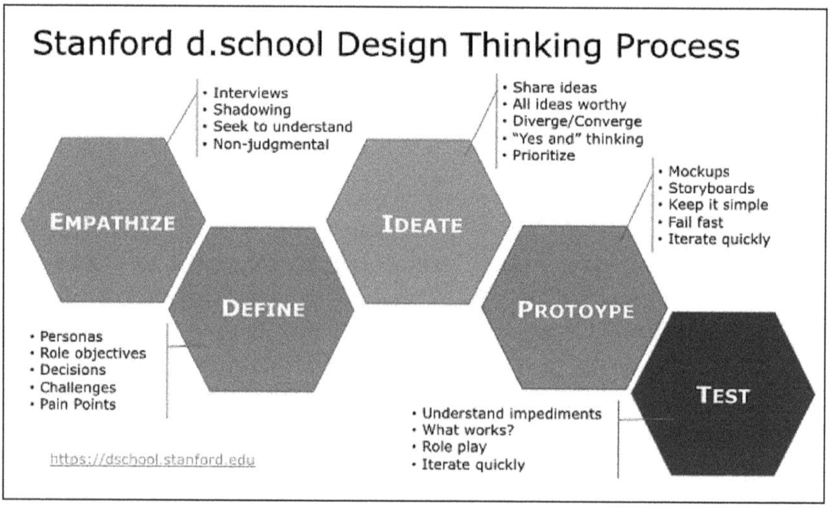

Figure 1: Design thinking is an iterative process. Source: Stanford d.school.

The beauty and simplicity of the methodology is that, by its nature, it requires participants to brainstorm to think big and wide before narrowing its scope, and then presses participants to create, test creation, and then recreate quickly. The idea here is that perfect is the enemy of good[2] and the development of good to great to best in class happens as you iterate and make small changes along the way. The front end of the design thinking process can be slow, but the second part – the prototyping, iterating, testing and recreating – should happen relatively quickly as you are never looking for perfection. Instead, applying a design thinking methodology suggests you are looking for a "good enough" place from which to start building and refining.

This alone is a huge step for the legal industry that by its nature is risk averse – preferring certainty over doubt. The legal industry would prefer to be stagnant and safe than to risk any sort of uncertainty. And while that certainly makes sense when it comes to making strategic transactional and litigious decisions for clients, it's not a school of thought that should also be applied to the daily operations of the business of law as it relates to running a firm or a department. Take, for example, the way a matter is brought into a firm. Conflict checking, ethical walls put in place where required, necessary parties informed and opening the file is a process that can often take days with long strings of approvals and oversight when it should only take hours or even minutes. Imagine the kind of time, money, resources and so on that a firm could save in reimagining its matter in-take process. Similarly, in a legal department, when a contract needs to be signed for the provision or procurements of goods, there is often a long drawn out process of contract vetting, approvals and back and forth with the vendors in a process that can be taxing and time consuming. What if you could take those two processes and completely reimagine them? What if you could get all the people, documents, processes and such in a room together for an afternoon and reimagine the way work is done? What if you could test your hypothesis in the moment and refine as you are documenting and considering how to implement the new process? How much faster and more engaged would people be in participating in a process or solution to a problem that resulted in something more flexible, easier, and more efficient? Design thinking by its nature does just that.

Design thinking holds the promise of a better way to solve big, complicated problems. I believe it is imperative for the legal industry to test some of its long-held systems and beliefs against the modern way of doing things. Only then can it learn what can be done better, particularly given the industry's unique nuances that can make design thinking difficult.

While empathy and truly understanding the audience is at the heart of every design thinking exercise and solution, it is the one of the hardest concepts for the legal industry to grapple with and embrace into its processes. Lawyers, and the legal industry, trade in fact and not feelings. This makes empathy a challenge in an industry that trades on memos and well thought out and researched opinions. Empathy can be taught and it can be learned through listening to hear, not to answer, and through other emotional intelligence strength training. I will save that discussion for another book. Instead, I want to focus on the other parts of the process and how those can be enhanced and executed on in the context of the legal industry. Below are three elements to consider in achieving balance and success as you work towards implementing design thinking as a problem-solving mechanism.

Problem definition – the complexity of the legal industry

Problems in the legal industry can be described as BHAP (borrowing from the term Big Hairy Audacious Goals – coined by Jim Collins and Jerry Porras in their book, *Built to Last: Successful Habits of Visionary Companies*) – a long-term, 10-to-25-year goal, guided by your company's core values and purpose. But it's more than just a goal. Big Hairy Audacious Problems[3] are the types of problems that are layered in minutiae, almost impossible to unravel like a hair ball, because law firms are highly matrixed organizations with distributed decision-making power. There is a dichotomy of fee earners, or those who bill clients for their time, and those who support the fee earners but are professionals or paraprofessionals in their own right. Often, administrative responsibility is the purview of the non-fee earners or allied professionals, but oversight of these functions is still maintained by the fee earners. In legal departments there are no fee earners, but the cost-center mentality still applies. It can get complicated and so too can the resulting problem definition, which is critical to the design thinking process.

Problems for fee-earners or stakeholders in the firm context may not be issues for the allied professionals or the legal department. The inefficiencies of one group may not worry another. Problems are not universal. Building on the example above, a lawyer may start working on a file for a client the moment he or she is engaged, not stopping to consider the several days' worth of approvals and administrative efforts that need to take place before the matter can actually be billed. Whose problem is that? Is it the lawyer's? Is it the client's who won't be properly billed? Records management? The legal assistant? In this scenario, where is the greatest sense of "pain" that needs to be addressed for the betterment of the entire organization? When engaging in design thinking methodology, the definition of the problem and its audience is critical for success. In the legal industry this can be the most challenging step – understanding whose problem you are trying to solve and how much of an impact the problem ultimately has on the business. But without this step properly defined, any resulting solution will have limited success and the outcome will be a sense that design thinking has failed to produce a solution to the problem you sought to resolve.

Silo breaking – equal airtime

As mentioned earlier, the legal industry is built on a bifurcated platform of fee earners and allied professionals. While in theory the two have a symbiotic relationship, in practice the two worlds can often operate in separate silos. To make matters worse, different practice areas with the same problems may not know of one another's issues, just as one support function may not know if or how another is impacted by the process of another. Put simply, law firms are full of autonomous groups that do not communicate or collaborate well with one another. Perspectives, points of view, and diversity of approach and thought can be lost or not shared as a result of the prevailing operating structures. That said, for design thinking solutions to come to the fore and have any material impact, for solutions to be implemented and adopted, it is incumbent upon the firm or department hosting a session to ensure the right people, from across the organization, be in the room. This doesn't mean you need to host dozens of people at a design thinking workshop but it does mean that you need to make sure all stakeholders are represented. This will ensure that you solve the right problem (once defined) in a way that will meet the needs of all stakeholders and that iterations can be tested by all of those who would engage with the solution or the problem.

Expert facilitation – making lawyers have fun

Lawyers are used to being right. They spend three years in school learning how to argue using fact and manipulation to mitigate risk and present a solid irrefutable position. Design thinking, by its unrestricted nature, does almost the complete opposite. Lawyers spend their days talking to clients and drafting agreements or researching precedent cases to inform litigation strategies. This work involves staring at a computer screen, poring over texts, or perhaps drafting with a pen on yellow legal-sized pads and arguing or refuting a position. Design thinking involves colored markers, Post-It notes in different shades, non-judgemental discussion, brainstorming, and drawing. It requires a strong hand to bring lawyers along and encourage their participation and comfort with the process.

The purpose of a good design thinking event is to let imagination be your guide and to consider all the possibilities in solving a problem, leaving preconceived ideas and former solutions or processes in the past. For lawyers, accountants, and other professionals who work in absolutes, this can be a difficult task to not only accomplish but to even engage with openly. Personalities and culture in the legal industry can be an impediment to design thinking. That said, lawyers can also be some of the most creative intellectual minds and tend to be wordsmiths who must consider all aspects of the future that could impact their clients. They are smart and savvy but they may need help applying those qualities in different ways. This is why, when attempting design thinking with lawyers, you need to ensure you have a strong facilitator guiding the discussion. This is likely to be more successful if you choose someone from outside your organization as there is a tendency to pay better attention and be more respectful to a guest than to family. In the same way that children are better behaved at school or with relatives rather than at home with parents, it's human nature. But since we know design thinking is most successful with all stakeholders at the table, lawyer voices need to be heard. A skilled facilitator can bring out those voices and help all the opinions in the room be heard and neutralized within the discussion, regardless of the person's role in the firm or the bifurcated structure. An excellent facilitator can also make the lawyers in the room who are used to being risk averse have fun with the new uncharted territory.

Legal departments are growing, alternative legal service providers are here to stay, technology from e-Discovery to document automation and platforms are invading the hallowed halls of law firms and Millennial or Gen-Z lawyers who can't recall life before the smartphone are taking on the ranks as associates. The legal industry as we have known it for the last century has undergone a fundamental change and is in the middle of a digital transformation. The industry, like all industries in a state of flux, is trying to solve big problems such as associate recruitment, allied professional retention, and innovating to stay relevant and manage competition. Design thinking is a tool the industry can use to help it move beyond what it knows and tap into what it doesn't know in order to approach these big problems. Design thinking is not straightforward and it doesn't follow a neat series of steps. It can be messy, it can be challenging, and it is never quite complete. It calls for constant iteration and testing. It involves color, crazy ideas, and collaboration across a broad cross-section of the industry. But design thinking, with its quick reflective style based in empathy and rooted in diversity of thought, is precisely what the legal industry needs to help it shed its old-fashioned and cautious way of thinking to embrace a more modern view of the world and its place in it.

References

1. https://angel.co/legal-tech-1
2. Voltaire, who quoted an Italian proverb in his *Dictionnaire philosophique* in 1770: «*Il meglio è l'inimico del bene*". https://en.wikipedia.org/wiki/Perfect_is_the_enemy_of_good
3. https://blog.growthinstitute.com/scale-up-blueprint/bhag-big-hairy-audacious-goal

Chapter 6:
Legal Lean Sigma® Design

Catherine Alman MacDonagh, JD, CEO and founder, Legal Lean Sigma Institute LLC

Improvement or design?

It may be an art form in and of itself to design or redesign new ways to improve processes, or to use process improvement to improve design thinking. By analogy, these processes are like a great studio producer that adjusts levels to bring a unique or even signature sound to a musical collaboration, or a chef that can take random ingredients and make a beautiful, delicious meal with flavors and textures complementing one other.

I have long been interested in innovation, and it's not just because I enjoy developing competitive advantages. It is immensely satisfying to create frameworks that make it easier for people to collaborate, do better work, and stop doing things that don't add value.

What our team has learned at the Legal Lean Sigma Institute is that no organization ever approaches the way they will change and evolve the same way as any other. This suggests that it will be up to us as trusted advisors, consultants, teachers, and facilitators that we must also continuously improve what we do and the way we do it.

In short, we view ourselves as innovators and designers who embrace continuous improvement. As the great W. Edwards Deming said, "I am forever learning and changing." We believe that it is vital to keep learning, growing, and trying new things. This includes adjusting levels in existing frameworks, like the producer does, or combining the ingredients we have available and creating a new dish that no one has ever made before.

One example of this Improve/Design combination is in the creation of Legal Lean Sigma®. While we did not invent either Lean or Six Sigma methodologies, concepts, or tools, we were the first to translate these tried and true manufacturing concepts and apply them to the legal space. In fact, we own the registered trademark in Legal Lean Sigma. It is, by definition, unique. That is partly because the ways we apply concepts and tools that come from industries like manufacturing to the way we do and deliver work in legal really are different. Is this considered improvement? Design? Or a combination of both?

Consider other examples of how we have combined improvement and design to create new approaches. After creating Legal Lean Sigma, we collaborated with others and added project management:

In short order, we collaborated to add project management. This made us the first (and remain the only) organization to teach and certify in process improvement and project management – in combination. This greatly facilitates the understanding and application of the two, as they ought to be employed.

Another way we applied process improvement and design thinking to our own work is our award-winning Legal WorkOut®. This original framework combines different process improvement, project management, and design thinking concepts and tools. We developed a completely new framework that enables cross-functional, cross-organizational, diverse teams of people to engage in a collaborative, accelerated approach to improving legal and business processes. It is designed to convert ideas into results in 30-90 days while also providing framework for longer-term improvement work.

Are these examples of process improvement? Or design thinking? The answer we propose is c) – both a) and b).

Perhaps a team doing innovation or improvement work requires a more rigorous framework, either throughout a project or for certain phases of it. Another may benefit from a lot of flexibility and freedom. The success of a process improvement practitioner is often dependent on picking the right tool for the situation at hand; why would we limit ourselves to using only one approach for everything? This work is never one size fits all. Each team, project, and organization is unique. What always produces success is to work flexibly within a tried and true structure (such as PI or DT).

Legal Lean Sigma Design™ takes a similar approach. Our most recent invention combines elements of traditional design thinking, then layers in Lean Sigma and project management methodologies and tools. The result is a unique approach that successfully combines complementary ingredients.

Background – a brief introduction to PI and PM

The Legal Lean Sigma® approach to process improvement (PI) and project management (PM) is based on the premise that efficiency should never be defined as simply "doing more with less".

Rather, efficiency involves determining what are the right things to do (Lean), ensuring that we have a good process for doing those things right (Six Sigma), and then managing projects so that we do those right things the right way, the first time, every time. When used in combination, there is a multiplier effect.

Lean
Do the Right Things
Simplify processes:

- Eliminate waste / steps;
- Maximize process speed; and
- Greatly improve productivity.

Focus on resource efficiency.

Six Sigma
Do Things Right
Understand relationships between variables.
Understand process capability and align with requirements.
Reduce /eliminate and control undesirable variation.

Consider this when determining which comes first and when to add the second: there is little point in being excellent at managing a terrible process. This includes the error many are making these days, which is to add technology to a process that has yet to be improved. A corollary, then, is that there is little value to having an optimized process that is not managed well. In combining PI and PM, our goals are:

- Increased productivity;
- Increased quality;
- Reduced costs;
- High client and user satisfaction;
- Improved employee engagement and morale; and
- Efficient work environment.

The processes of DT and PI (yes, PI is a process!)

Design thinking is a process that helps us develop practical and innovative solutions. DT takes place in this order: Empathize, Define, Ideate, Prototype, Test, Implement.

There are several different types of processes one can employ in doing process improvement work. Regardless, we always examine any describable, repeatable sequence of activities that generates an outcome – this includes the way we create and deliver value to the client and the embodiment of our knowledge as to (ideally) the best way to do something, not just pain points.

We analyze the current state, search for issues, problems and opportunities, then employ tools and techniques to address priorities, then improve and lock in the new process.

The classic frameworks for doing process improvement work are DMAIC – an acronym for the sequence Define, Measure, Analyze, Improve, Control – and DMADV – Define, Measure, Analyze, Design, Verify framework.

Lean focuses on creating simpler, faster processes. Six Sigma is a methodology for controlling variation and reducing defects down to fewer than 3.4 per million opportunities.

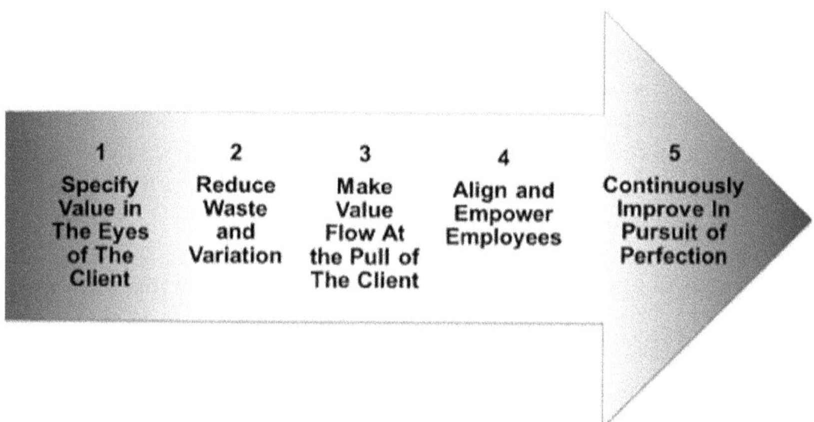

Figure 1: The five key principles of Lean Sigma.

Lean Sigma rests on a series of five key principles; they are observed in a specific sequence:

1. Specify value in the eyes of the client – this means focus on the client and understand exactly what the client requires in terms of work product and service delivery.
2. Reduce waste (Lean) and variation (Six Sigma) – some "natural variation" is desirable and we want that flexibility in our processes;

we are interested in reducing if not eliminating "special cause" or undesirable variation.

3. Make value flow at the pull of the client – this simply means that our processes and people must be able to provide what the client wants, the way the client wants it, when the client wants it.
4. Align and empower employees – involve people from different roles and levels of management. We always work with cross-functional, diverse teams.
5. Continuously improve in pursuit of perfection – this means we do not wait for waste and undesirable variation to negatively impact people and processes. They may become the standard because "that's the way we've always done that here." It is important to be flexible and thorough.

Process improvement frameworks – DMAIC and DMADV

DMAIC (Define, Measure, Analyze, Improve, Control) is an approach to understanding and then improving an existing process or product. It is a framework that focuses on making adjustments and controlling something that already exists. The objective is to improve quality, speed, and/or cost.

- **Define** the problem and why it needs to be solved.
- **Measure** the current performance of the process.
- **Analyze** the opportunities to reduce waste or variation.
- **Improve** the process by identifying, implementing and validating process changes.
- **Control** the process by implementing methods to ensure improvements will be sustainable.

DMADV (Define, Measure, Analyze, Design, Validate (Verify), on the other hand, is a method that aims to design a new product, or to radically redesign an existing process or product that is problematic. Those steps are also observed in a particular sequence:

- **Define** the process or product to be developed.
- **Measure**: Agree on key performance indicators and determine the baseline performance of the process.

- **Analyze**: Identify performance goals and determine how process inputs affect process outputs.
- **Design:** Test and optimize the process to deliver what the client(s) require(s).
- **Validate/verify** that the new process/product is able to deliver what the client requires.

DMADV is designed to prevent problems from happening by employing quality and robust design concepts. The focus is on creating the right product or process correctly the first time. The DMADV approach appears to initially follow the first three steps of DMAIC but diverges in the last two steps by introducing Design/Redesign and Validate/Verify to gain the improvements needed.

As such, there may not appear to be a major difference between DMAIC and DMADV. The first three steps are similar, but notice the subtleties in their differences. They are not identical and the last two steps are quite different. In fact, the differences between DMAIC and DMADV are quite significant.

With DMADV, the design and verify stages are employed to enhance client and stakeholder satisfaction. In other words, unlike DMAIC, which improves a process based on client requirements, DMADV allows us to revisit the design based on end-user suggestions and input. Accordingly, the design can be restructured to please the client(s). They will verify that the design that has been implemented works for them.

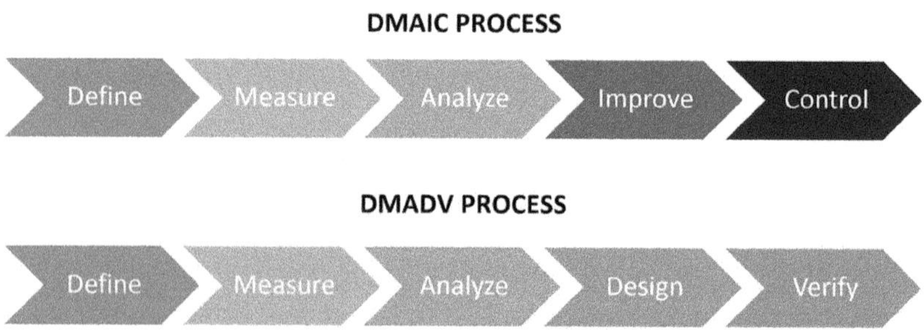

Figure 2: DMAIC process and DMADV process.

With DMADV, the Design and Verify steps deal with redesigning a process to match customer needs, as opposed to the Improve and Control steps that focus on determining ways to readjust and control the process.

With regards to measurement, DMAIC measures the current performance of a process. Control systems are established with DMAIC in order to keep check on the business' future performance.

While DMAIC is focused on improving a current process that isn't meeting client/customer needs and/or specifications, DMADV is often employed with new services and products. With more of us in legal creating new things rather than improving something that already exists, it is an increasingly useful methodology. In other words, when there is no existing product or service, DMADV may be the best framework for us to employ. It may also also be a good choice when a process improvement either doesn't work at all or doesn't work as well as expected.

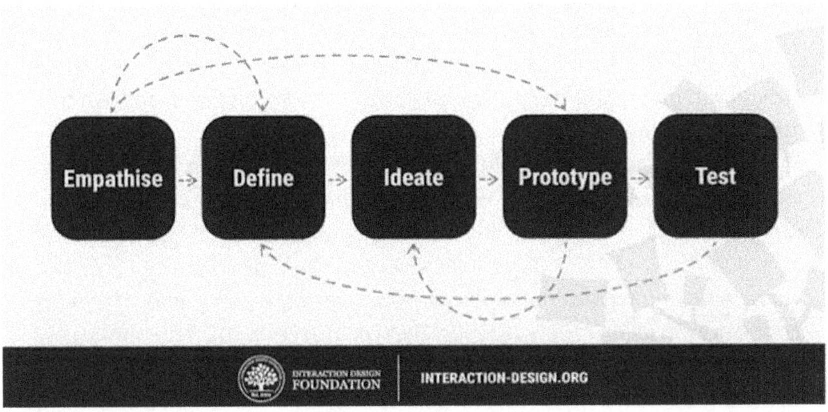

Figure 3: Design thinking – a five-stage process. This version of the design thinking process is one that reflects the iterative nature of the work; this shows the contrast to the more sequential nature of process improvement frameworks.

Combining the DT, DMAIC and DMADV processes

Step one of DMAIC and DMADV – Define and (DT) Empathize

The design thinking process begins with Empathize, while the DMAIC and DMADV models both start with the Define phase.

Interestingly, in the three models we always begin our work by understanding and defining what the client needs and wants. This enables us to deliver an outcome that meets those needs. DMAIC and DMADV start by defining client requirements. By creating an objective specification, with measurable parameters, we develop specific benchmarks to track our progress. When we combine the client requirements in Define with the insights acquired through Empathize, we create an even more useful measurement and guideline by which to apply our work.

A close cousin to client requirements is found in DT's Empathize work. Design in our world might be considered to facilitate our ability to build legal systems and services that are more human-centered, usable, and satisfying.

As outlined in *An Introduction to Design Thinking: Process Guide*[3] by Hasso Plattner at the Institute of Design at Stanford:

> *"Empathy is the centerpiece of a human-centered design process. The Empathize mode is the work you do to understand people, within the context of your design challenge. It is your effort to understand the way they do things and why, their physical and emotional needs, how they think about the world, and what is meaningful to them.*
>
> *"As a design thinker, the problems you are trying to solve are rarely your own – they are those of a particular group of people; in order to design for them, you must gain empathy for who they are and what is important to them.*
>
> *"Observing what people do and how they interact with their environment gives you clues about what they think and feel. It also helps you learn about what they need. By watching people, you can capture physical manifestations of their experiences – what they do and say. This will allow you to infer the intangible meaning of those experiences in order to uncover insights. These insights give you direction to create innovative solutions. The best solutions come out of the best insights into human behavior. But learning to recognize those insights is harder than you might think. Why? Because our minds automatically filter out a lot of information without our even realizing it. We need to learn to see things "with a fresh set of eyes," and empathizing is what gives us those new eyes.*
>
> *"Engaging with people directly reveals a tremendous amount about the way they think and the values they hold. Sometimes these thoughts and values are not obvious to the people who hold them, and a good conversation can surprise both the designer and the subject by the unanticipated insights that are revealed. The stories that people tell and the things that people say they do – even if they are different from what they actually do – are strong indicators of their deeply held beliefs about the way the world is. Good designs are built on a solid understanding of these beliefs and values."*

The initial phase in Lean Sigma requires that we define "quality" from the point of clients. This is challenging – each client defines quality differently; however, we must measure quality in a similar way that our clients do. While we typically consider "clients" to be external to our department or organization, when we do this work, we consider any user of the process to be a client. That is because all processes exist to serve clients.

For example, when designing a process that feeds components to another in-house process, such as intake or onboarding, the primary clients of the process are internal (e.g. an onboarding lateral), while the secondary clients are external (e.g. the clients of an onboarding lateral).

Obviously, the best sources for this information are the clients themselves. Too often, we do not ask and, when we do, we do not get specific enough information about what the client really wants. It is useful to understand what are the upper and lower levels of acceptability that the client has for the work product and the service expected/delivered.

I often use toast as the example when explaining the range of acceptability. If the bread is not toasted enough it is out of range. If it is toasted too much, it is also out of range. Somewhere in the middle is the degree of doneness that the client to whom we are serving toast will accept. The more expert we claim to be, the narrower the range from the client's perspective.

For example, one expects perfect toast when at a luxury hotel. The bread will not only be toasted to the right degree, but it will also be presented beautifully and delivered with impeccable service. Overly cooked toast and less than stellar service does not work in that scenario.

Consider that the same customer is being served toast in a different situation altogether. This time, it is created and delivered by a child as a birthday present to a parent. The range of acceptability (for most people) is going to be significantly wider, both for the product (the toast) and the service as well.

Combining the concepts and tools of Empathize and Define allows the exact upper us to get specific information that facilitates our ability to determine the upper and lower limits, and thus the range, of acceptability. Does the client want condiments? What about slicing the toast – triangles? Or rectangles? What about a beverage? Or will a toasted piece of bread, served uncut, without condiments do just fine? Consider how often we overproduce based on what we *think* the client wants or needs versus what the client *actually* wants or needs.

If we do not have this type of clarity for every project and each process, we will not really know if we are performing to the client's specifications. This means that we fail to be "client focused" or "client centered", as so many law firms claim. With more operations and procurement professionals defining specific standards, it is increasingly important to understand the range of acceptability as well as how well we are doing at delivering to those standards.

Information that can be used to define what the client needs might also come from business and competitive intelligence sources. This may be in the form of industry research, historical data, and reports.

Regardless of source, our objective is to have our design be focused on what the client both needs and is willing to pay for.

Step two of DMAIC and DMADV – Measure

The second step of DMAIC and DMADV is to create the specification(s) based on what the clients/customers want. The specification describes the product or service in a way that is measurable, allowing data to be collected and compared with the specified requirements.

In the Measure phase, we gain a thorough understanding of the process through process mapping and data-gathering. Our work involves establishing a baseline of performance against which to measure progress; we measure the process to identify waste in the process (Lean) and variation, defects, and causes of defects (Six Sigma). Since we can't possibly improve everything at once, one output of this phase is prioritized areas of opportunity for improvement as a limited number of focus areas.

As in the earlier toast example, this work is essential for ensuring the final product meets the customer's needs. It is why we think it makes sense to include Measure in our combined version of Legal Lean Sigma® Design.

Processes have a "characteristic performance level" and "characteristic resource requirements". The process performance / process capability describes how well the process meets client expectations. Process resource requirement / process efficiency refers to the resources (time, people, equipment, money) required to carry out the process. There are many dimensions along which a process can be measured; a process can perform well in some dimensions and poorly in others.

As such, in this step, there are categories of characteristics to be measured. These are:

- Critical to Quality (CTQ) – these are quality parameters that directly relate to the customer's needs, typically in the areas of speed, quality, and cost.
- Process capability – how capable is the process of delivering what the client(s) need(s)?
- Resource requirements – what are the resources required to carry out the process?

- Risk assessments – what are the risks and how can they be measured? For example, what are the regulatory requirements the product must meet? Are there measurable standards? What is the schedule that must be met, and what are appropriate milestones?
- Product capabilities – establish the ways to measure how well the product meets client needs.
- Service capabilities – establish the ways to measure how well the service meets client needs.

If DMAIC and DMADV are used to improve an existing process or product, as improvements are made, the progress from the existing condition toward the desired characters can then be measured.

The Measure phase involves understanding *what* is happening in our processes. It is important to have quality and quantify of data for an improvement team to make decisions about what it will select as "focus areas" – a shortlist of prioritized areas into which it will delve more deeply in the Analyze phase.

In other words, to identify root causes of waste and variation (the work performed in the Analyze phase), understanding the current state of the process is critical. As such, from a Lean Sigma perspective, our understanding of the process must be deep and extensive. This requires an abundance of detailed data about the process.

Since data collection in the Lean Sigma process includes interviewing people, taking observations, and asking questions, our model incorporates the Measure phase and combines it with the first step of DT – Empathize – with the first step in our new Legal Lean Sigma Design model.

Step three of DMAIC and DMADV – Analyze

At this stage, in both approaches, the proposed process or product is analyzed and studied to determine whether there are better ways to achieve the desired results. Areas that need adjustment or improvement, both in the product and the process of making the product, are identified.

In the Analyze phase, we examine each focus area to identify and verify waste, defects, and determine root causes.

Root cause analysis takes place in three steps – exploring, generating hypotheses, and verifying causes. We use the data gathered in the Measure phase to find patterns, trends, and other differences that suggest or support theories about the causes of waste or defects. Notably, we may need to gather further data to complete our analysis.

By examining our focus areas for bottlenecks, disconnects, and redundancies that might contribute to waste, and analyzing data to understand potential root causes of problems and defects, an improvement team can develop root cause hypotheses for problems. We can then investigate and verify root cause hypotheses to isolate the "vital few" root causes.

This work is not typically included in design thinking. Our experience shows us that Analyze helps us determine *why* waste and variation are occurring. If we skip this, we might (probably) be designing in a way that addresses symptoms rather than root causes.

Step four of DMADV – Design, step four of DMAIC – Improve, and Step 3, 4 and 5 of Design Thinking – Ideate, Prototype, and Test

At this point, the people who have been eager to start solving are more than ready to begin to transition from learning about the problems and the clients to coming up with solutions.

Using DMA**D**V and DMA**I**C, we will now **D**esign or **I**mprove the new process or product. The team generates creative solutions that address the root causes confirmed in the Analyze phase. The step involves designing, testing, and implementing ideas.

The rigor of process improvement work involves following the framework without skipping steps. As such, there is even a process to generating solutions. This involves developing problem statements and solution filters/specifications, and then engaging in structured brainstorming, using approaches such as analogy, channeling, and the ever-popular anti-solution. After that, we develop solution ideas by combining solutions, challenging assumptions, and making creative ideas practical.

To select the best solution, we first determine what will pass through our solution filter; if a solution does not meet our specifications, we can figure out whether there is a way to do so, but otherwise, we move on to others that will. Then, we use a variety of tools such as force field analysis, pros and cons, weighted decision matrix, and impact/ease matrix to select and prioritize the solutions that get recommended by the team.

While wild ideas are always encouraged, process improvement structures provide linear, logical approaches to process improvement work. For that reason alone, they are quite useful in doing innovation work in legal.

The Ideate step of DT appears to have a lot in common with the Design phase of DMADV and the Improve Phase of DMAIC. However, design thinking, while certainly structured, is far less constraining. It obviously works well as it produces so many breakthrough ideas and products. One theory is that because the approach involves the team challenging the norm, there are less cultural constraints than those that currently exist in law. However, that is changing rapidly!

So, while Ideate may be quite a bit looser in its construct than the Improve phase (it is usually what people associate with design thinking – pipe cleaners, Legos, a fun, bright environment), at a high level, the step still involves generating ideas and solutions. Out of the box type thinking and creativity are encouraged. Teams are supposed to move as quickly as they can from the "how might we?" questions that begin DT into prototyping and making ideas "real" to begin testing (and failing quickly to learn faster).

Whether using PI or DT, the goal is to generate a quantity of ideas rather than quality initially.

Whether we call this step Design, Improve, or Ideate, here is where we will build our prototype, try it out, develop pilot plans and see how it works, learn, iterate, and learn (it's listed twice deliberately).

Design thinking involves Testing, which is similar in theory and practice to piloting improvement ideas. It is important to test improvements and designs with actual users. This way, we can collect feedback, which is what enables the solutions to actually solve the problems they were supposed to address.

Sometimes, testing will reveal that the team has made assumptions or failed to consider realistic conditions during the previous phases. Testing may highlight that processes that appear to be performing well actually are not. This produces an iteration and the team will develop new prototypes to address user feedback. As such, the prototyping and testing phases are a cycle that continues until the project is complete.

This may be an excellent approach where the organization and the users have a high degree of resiliency or tolerance for experimentation. However, that does not describe the majority of the world's law firms or legal departments. This is where we can make, perhaps, the most compelling case for introducing some of the concepts and tools of process improvement and project management. If we have done our work in Define, Measure, and Analyze, it is likely we will have fewer assumptions or failures to consider conditions in which the user functions.

In process improvement, when we are ready for full scale implementation, we will engage in detailed action planning, communication, training, troubleshooting, measurement and a lot of change management. This is extremely important in a legal environment, where even minor errors can produce major problems. It is important for the improvement/design team, as well as the project sponsors, owners, and leaders to have confidence in the new, redesigned process or product. A key element of good project management applies here: NO SURPRISES.

This takes us to our last phase in process improvement and design thinking.

Step five of DMADV – Validate (Verify), DMAIC (Control) and step six of Design Thinking (Implement)

The last phases in DMADV and DMAIC involve Verifying that the result meets or exceeds the client's requirements and Controlling the new process. The team develops approaches to maintain a process with a stable, predictable operation that meets client requirements.

The work in process improvement includes documenting the process with standard operating procedures and creating a project repository. Control design and process ownership are instituted. Finally, a process improvement project concludes when improvements have been translated into benefits.

These steps are ongoing; even after the new process is implemented and/or the product is released, client feedback should be encouraged and incorporated into future designs. The desired result is to have a product that perfectly meets the client's requirements. In the law, we want to deliver our work and our service within the acceptable range. This way, we neither underperform nor overproduce.

Designers are also trying to develop the best possible solutions *for their users*. It's not helpful to determine the success of a design by any other metric, even if the design is incredibly clever or unique or the most creative. Clients/users care about solutions that solve their problems or help them seize opportunities.

Employing a combined process improvement and design thinking framework facilitates a design or improvement team's ability to determine what clients/users consider the optimal solution, rather than make decisions based on their own biases. If we are not improving and designing to create satisfied clients and users, what are we doing and why are we doing it?

Summary – improving the DT process with PI / redesigning PI with DT

As claims IDEO:

> *"In employing design thinking, you're pulling together what's desirable from a human point of view with what is technologically feasible and economically viable. It also allows those who aren't trained as designers*

to use creative tools to address a vast range of challenges. The process starts with taking action and understanding the right questions. It's about embracing simple mindset shifts and tackling problems from a new direction."[4]

Legal Lean Sigma® Design is the only methodology in general and in legal in particular that 1) integrates aspects of traditional design thinking plus the DMAIC and DMADV processes, and then 2) adds foundational legal project management and change management techniques, including the critical preparation steps prior to engaging in these activities, that are particularly fundamental to success in the unique environment of the legal profession.

Legal Lean Sigma® Design is a distinct approach to improvement and design work that works well in law offices of all kinds. In effect, it is an example of how we can use process improvement and project management to improve classic design thinking. It is also an example of how design thinking. It is also an example of how design thinking is used to make process improvement methodologies.

Once a producer gains experience and knows how to record and mix sound, or a chef has learned what ingredients complement and balance each other, it becomes easier to try new things and learn from them. And so it is with the process improvement, project management, and design thinking work we do. We use these combined frameworks and tools to create signature sounds and dishes that are unique to each organization. This is how we deliver greater value via human-centered design while simultaneously creating competitive advantages.

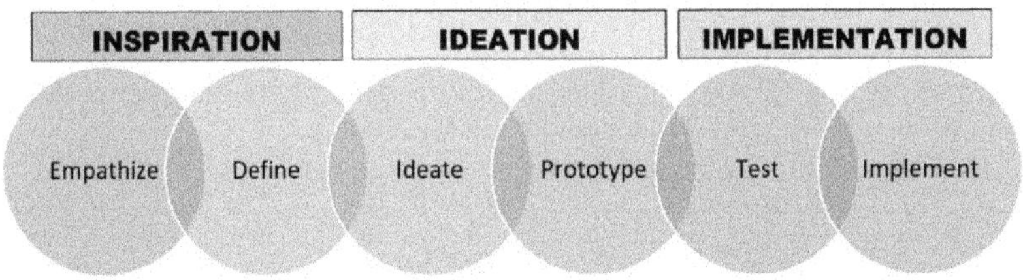

Figure 4: The design thinking process.

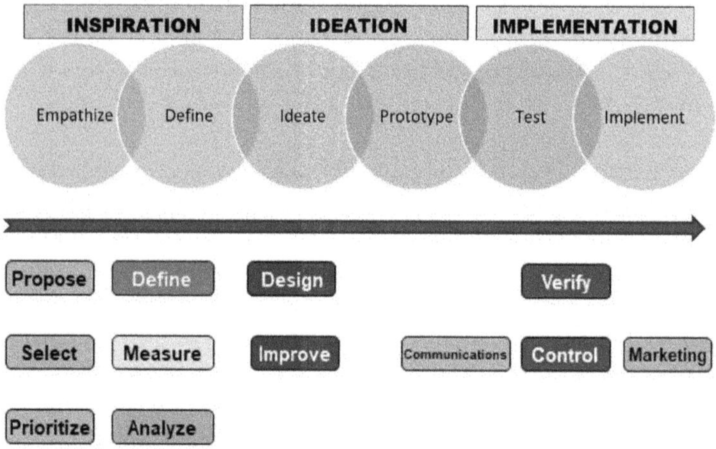

Figure 5: Combined design thinking, DMAIC and DMADV processes.

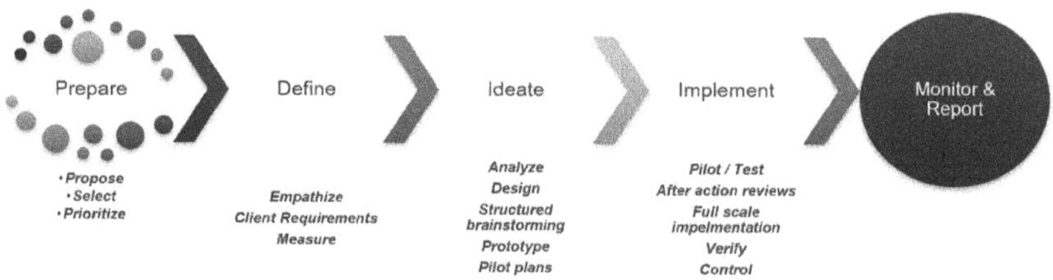

Figure 6: Legal Lean Sigma Design™ process.

References

1. www.sixsigmadaily.com/six-sigma-sixty-customer-needs-and-requirements/
2. Six Sigma Daily at www.sixsigmadaily.com/dmaic-vs-dmadv-what-is-the-difference/
3. https://dschool-old.stanford.edu/sandbox/groups/designresources/wiki/36873/attachments/74b3d/ModeGuideBOOTCAMP2010L.pdf
4. www.ideou.com/blogs/inspiration/what-is-design-thinking

Chapter 7:

From enthusiasm to execution – the growing legal design community

By Josh Kubicki, co-founder and design principal, Bold Duck Studio

Is legal design bullsh*t? Now is the time to answer this. While the design community within the legal market is still relatively small, it is time to turn the lens onto ourselves. Reality checks and critique are the accelerants of maturity. If the growing number of design enthusiasts in legal want to be taken seriously by their organizations, deepen their capabilities, and speed up adoption, they need to pivot from revelry of events to demonstration of evidence. We need to temper the celebrations and amplify the measurements.

Over the last decade, design has become quite popular across the global economy as organizations seek to find new ways to grow and strengthen their ability to innovate. It has become a management trend to help spark innovation and more effective problem-solving. Large incumbent companies like IBM, Ford, Infosys, Capital One, 3M, UnitedHealth Group, Pepsico and many others have invested heavily in design talent and programs. High growth start-ups such as Airbnb, Pinterest, Kickstarter, Blue Apron and Buzzfeed all have founders that come from a design background. The large consulting and strategy firms, McKinsey, IBM, EY, PWC, Deloitte, BCG, KMPG and Accenture have been acquiring design agencies at a quickening pace. And not just one or two, we are talking five or six each over the last several years. Rigorous academic studies are presenting evidence that design thinking is central to solving significant world problems; issues such as global warming, disease, and terrorism among others. Design is certainly having a moment.

With any management and business trend there comes the inevitable backlash and contrarian movements. These are healthy as they help flesh out what is real and works from what is pure vanity and vapor.

In 2017, Natasha Jen, an award-winning designer, stepped on stage at one of the design industry's more notable events to give a talk called

"Design Thinking is Bullsh*t". Beyond the provocative title, her remarks sparked a fierce debate across the global design community. This tension is best summed up as this. Seasoned designers surround themselves with evidence. Newcomers embrace decorations. Seasoned designers define their value based on output. Newcomers base it on input. Seasoned designers remain students. Newcomers proclaim expertise. The potency of this framing is that it crystallized the growing tension between seasoned designers and newcomers as to what design thinking is and isn't. This is not an academic question. As design thinking sweeps through all industries and markets, it is an important question to answer.

The notion of design thinking, no matter how pivotal towards innovation and problem-solving, is also a field of controversies. It carries with it conflicting definitions and misconceived notions of creative tools for superficial cure-all solutions to address deeply rooted structural challenges. It begs for clear definitions and clarity of purpose. This is something that even seasoned experts, like Natasha and a host of others, struggle to do.

Perhaps the best way to sum this up is the following quote from Bruce Nussbaum, professor of innovation and design at Parsons The New School for Design and the former assistant managing editor for *Business Week*. When speaking about design, he had this to say about the general understanding of what it is: "CEOs and top managers hate the word design as they associate it with… curtains, wallpaper, and maybe their suits."

That pretty much nails it. The buzz and hype coupled with the interdisciplinary nature of design creates a high degree of suspicion and confusion for any newcomer. Putting newcomers aside, when lawyers first hear about design, their natural and well-honed analytical tendencies kick in and simply cannot grasp what design is or why they should care.

For clarity then, here is a helpful way to think about design and design thinking.

Lawyers are typically associated with analytical thinking. This is a way of approaching a situation and solving problems using logic, facts, and objective reasoning. It seeks to eliminate extraneous information and dissect information into simpler elements. Law school teaches future lawyers to "think like a lawyer", meaning that the student learns how to break down complex fact patterns, identify legal issues, apply appropriate legal rules, and then articulate a clear position on how a situation should be resolved.

Analytical thinking is not the sole province of lawyers, obviously. In fact, many people think this way, maybe just not as well-honed or as well-practiced as a lawyer.

In design, the thinking construct emphasizes creative thinking over analytical thinking, but involves both. Design begins with divergent exploration. Its lens is not fact-based, it is experience-based. This means designers do not accept a situation as it is described – they seek to live the challenge as the person who encounters it does. Design uses empathy as a way to force a new perspective; one gained from exploring the problem as the actual person experiencing it, rather than an outside observer. The goal here is to discover the right way to think about the problem, removing biases and solution-jumping. Ultimately, design tends to uncover unmet needs that, if met, will better and more holistically address the original problem.

Put more simply – analytical thinking is about finding the right answers. Design is about finding the right questions.

Now design thinking. Design thinking is simply the exercise of thinking like a designer. Anyone can do it, just like anyone can think analytically. There are various methods to use and exercises to instigate this type of thinking. And they tend to be fairly straightforward or even obvious once explained. But thinking or behaving like a designer and actually designing something are two very different things. Just like *being* a lawyer compared to *thinking* like a lawyer are two very different things. Design thinking is a way for people to experience the design mindset and process. It is a pathway to execution but does not represent execution itself.

Another quick analogy. If you are an architect, you may use design thinking to uncover a new approach to creating truly accessible buildings that allow for seamless and easy movement for the physically impaired. You might land on an amazing construct that promises a seamless and fluid experience for any human, regardless of physical capability. Now you have to build it! It has to be designed within the bounds of physical materials, local ordinances, and so on. That is design. Making the idea real based on both the possibilities *and* constraints of the environment in which the idea will live.

But why does this matter to lawyers?

Just being a good solid lawyer has quickly become table stakes in many practice areas across the market. Clients have many choices when looking to outside providers and many of those options look the same. This results in many traditional practice areas becoming more challenging to compete within and remain profitable as competition increases, price pressures mount, new providers emerge, and client demands intensify and change.

Throughout any multi-practice firm, partners are serving and interacting with diverse client segments. Each segment has its own unique characteristics that impact how the client buys, interacts, and works with the partner, practice group, and firm. Most firms are managing a diverse set of client segments. Some practices may be serving certain clients within the so-called middle market, while other groups have more global and sophisticated clients who demand new and different capabilities, services, and products from their service providers. While there are still practice areas that can operate within the more traditional platform of a law firm, more and more firms are experiencing the pressure to respond to market changes by augmenting or completely overhauling certain practice group business models.

This is creating significant structural, cultural, and financial stress within firms as they struggle to operate the existing business platform of the firm while they also explore, test, and launch new models. Most are therefore unable to create the necessary purpose-built business practices, talent and capabilities, and client and provider experiences that would strengthen service delivery and client value in specific practice areas.

Too many law firms have been struggling to realize this and respond to it. Many want to ignore the signs of failing practice areas or subpar performance. Many more simply lack the tools and knowledge to detect these weaknesses and address them properly. Too many law firms are consistently squandering opportunities to create value for their clients and themselves. They are literally leaving money on the table. Serious money.

Competitive advantage

The simple fact is that too many law firms are confused as to what business they are in. It is nobody's fault. The lens under which the law firm business model is viewed has not changed in decades. Law firms generally define their business by referring to legal talent. "We have the best lawyers." Clients reinforce this with the common refrain, "We hire the lawyer, not the law firm".

Do you play to win? If you want to win in the marketplace you need competitive advantage, something that sets you apart from your competitors. Winning means that you are achieving your goals in the market – which can be profitability, attracting top brands as clients, client retention and growth – or you are a talent magnet attracting the truly best and brightest in certain areas. If you simply want to play and run with the pack, you can get by, but you will not prosper, nor will you survive over the long term. Rumor has it many partners are doing the latter right now – this is referred to as running out the clock.

Obtaining competitive advantage is neither as simple as a marketing campaign nor as mysterious as some dark art. It requires knowledge of a business' strategy, capabilities, and resources. The reason to focus on defining and creating a competitive advantage is that it allows organizations to enjoy a favorable position in the market. A position that can yield greater profit, more clients, and a differentiation that is difficult to replicate by competitors.

I am not one to argue the merits of disruption or transformation within the legal markets. Rather, I view it as a decision each law firm must make for itself based on how it wants to serve the markets it chooses. There is plenty of traditional legal work to go around for traditionally-minded clients providing abundant growth for many firms. To win, however, it is becoming more challenging to remain homogenous and simply claim the "best lawyers" as the core value proposition. Rather, it is apparent that a focus on defining a unique, or at least compelling, competitive advantage is quickly become a necessity. Yes, even in this traditional arena.

For the growing portion of work that can be addressed through non-traditional means and for the clients that are acclimated to a progressive approach, defining and delivering a unique competitive advantage for a practice group is in one regard easier but, in another vein, more challenging. It is easy in the sense that most progressive clients will willingly embrace active collaboration and exploration with the firm. Their expectation that a firm has all the answers on how to approach service delivery in a new way will not be very high. They will want to lean in with the firm and co-design a solution that fits as many needs for the client and the firm as possible. The more difficult challenge is in the actual design and delivery of the new solution.

Legal as a business

It is common practice to refer to law firms as partnerships and professional service firms. While these terms are somewhat accurate and fine to use in the normal course of dialogue, they become opaque and ambiguous when examining how strategy and competitive advantage can be created for a law firm.

When getting more specific, many people will refer to firms as service businesses, because they generate value *during* transactions and interactions with clients (providing services), rather than generating value *prior* to an interaction/transaction, as in manufacturing a product to be sold later in a store. But this is an incomplete definition.

To truly pinpoint what the firm is doing and what type of business it is requires an accounting of all of its components and, here is the key, *who* uses these components and for *what* purpose.

Large law firms typically have two broad functions – the legal practice and business operations.

The legal practice component is populated with the people and resources necessary to actually serve and work with clients. This component consists of lawyers and other fee-earners. This is the component that clients generally think they are buying. This component is typically organized by practice group, specialty team, geography, and in some cases, by specific matters. Large law firms house multiple and diverse service practice groups and specialty teams. Each of these teams and groups has its own strategy (articulated or not) and, whether it is recognized or not, is either aligned, irrelevant, or distracting to the overall firm strategy.

When looked at critically, each of these groups and teams are actually businesses in-and-of-themselves. They possess all of the elements of a complete business model, which for review are basically skills provided through services that solve distinct challenges for a defined set of clients who pay for these services.

As such, large law firms are housing dozens, if not hundreds, of small to large businesses. Yes, these distinct practice groups and specialty teams are in essence real businesses. Just so few people think of them in these terms.

Legal operations

The other main component of a law firm – business operations – is populated with the people and resources necessary to actually run and operate a large business such as a law firm. It generally consists of IT, HR, Finance, Marketing, Operations, Facilities, Administration and other business functions. While these are tailored towards the legal services market, they perform similar functions as their peers across the business landscape.

Collectively, the business functions are interrelated and interact across many lines of work. Clients do not typically think they are buying this part of the firm, but that does not mean that these functions do not interact or influence the service experience of the client. They do. But for cost reduction, most firms seldom look to the business side of the firm for competitive advantage, focusing almost exclusively on the legal practice component. Within legal operations can be found powerful tools, essential capabilities, and valuable experience across most of the business functions. Teams from practice management to docket, from conflicts to marketing – all have people with skills, experience, and perspective. They also can impact everything from operational soundness and efficiency to client sentiment and retention. This collective group of resources needs to be active in helping drive the firm towards growth – either directly or indirectly. No longer is it an option to treat this group, or for this group to behave, as though they are disconnected from the firm strategy. Most of the highest performing organizations engage and utilize their talent up and down and throughout the hierarchy. They must, to compete. They have realized that talent is a strategic differentiator – all talent. Law firms are no different. Many people need to be reminded of this – both on the legal side and on the operations side of the legal profession.

The practice/operations divide

Unfortunately, the operations side has been historically undernourished, underutilized and undervalued – creating a self-fulfilling prophecy of apathy and mediocrity that plagues many individuals and teams on this side of the market. It is uncommon to find a law firm that actively invests in its operational talent as though it is a material component of its success and therefore accountable for generating results.

Why is this? It is easy to devolve into a blame game that points to cultural differences and outdated beliefs, but these approaches are generally unhelpful. Yes, there are some material cultural drivers, but the key challenge can be summed up as this: lawyers tend to underestimate or are unaware of the scope, complexity, and importance of the business functions of a law firm, while the operational talent tends to slip into a servant mindset (passive and reacting) rather than a growth mindset (active and provoking) – forgoing the opportunities to generate value for the firm and better understand what its lawyers are facing in terms of competition and demands. In short, neither side truly understands one another.

Leading firms have already begun shifting or adding investments into generating more operational agility and engagement. Gaining or even maintaining ground within the legal market is requiring new approaches to thinking about how a firm operates, practice group strategy, and how to generate real competitive advantage that will stick.

Why design matters to legal

There is a lot of hype and buzz around innovation generally right now. Innovation is all too often portrayed as something that can be instantaneously created either by buying technology or by experimenting with design thinking. Innovation is nothing more than an outcome. It is not a discipline. It is not a practice. Innovation emerges out of the rigor required to surface unmet customer/user needs as well as the design of a business model that an organization can profit from and sustainably deliver. Instead, many teams focus on buying technology to solve a problem or create a PR opportunity. New software, a new process, or even a new kind of talent (like the emerging innovation-related titles) are what most are focusing on in their effort to generate more competitive advantage or value. The problem is that, regardless of the device used (tech, process, or talent), the culture in which these things will exist must be considered, pre-conditioned to accept and adopt this new development, and prepared to allow complete integration into the systems and practices of the organization. Ignoring this creates a high probability of failure. It is why so few organizations can pull off real measurable innovation.

With all this interest and activity in innovation, it only makes sense that design thinking has emerged within the legal market recently. But the design community within legal is nascent, even though it appears to be growing. There are only a few seasoned practitioners with significant numbers of design cycles who have been around long before the recent spike in enthusiasm. Most of the energy and evangelism is coming from relative newcomers. They may lack experience, but they have been exposed to the promise and process of design. They are introducing it to their organizations through design thinking events such as jam sessions and design sprints. The seduction of design is that it appears to be based on common sense and the Golden Rule – to be empathetic and treat others as you want to be treated. For business especially this makes sense but proves insanely challenging to pull off with every client and customer interaction. So, the promise of design resonates deeply. The way design thinking is described and exercised makes it feel accessible. Its process invites activity, not study.

Newcomers' practice of design tends to gravitate towards the visual portrayals of the front-end process itself – generating ideas and "solutions". This limited focus leads to outcomes that are highly conceptual and lack any real relevance to the business or the lawyers who run it. Seldom are they encountering or gaining experience with the backend of design where the idea gets stress-tested and runs directly into cultural, operational and political barriers.

Design is not always fun. It can be alienating, ugly, and slippery. Design is not always a team event. It can be isolating, lonely, and frustrating.

Design is not always about empathy. It is as much about intuition as it is experimentation. Empathy gets you off "go" but seldom takes you all the way around the board.

Design is a visually enabled methodology that lends itself to be represented by whiteboard doodles, post-it notes or legos. Let's be clear. Those things are tools, not solutions. Design is enhanced by an ability to visually represent certain things, but a design is improved not by doodling but by enduring cycles of research, observation, communication (as in writing and speaking), and interactions.

The essence of the "bullsh*t" question is that far too many people are only focusing on the front-end of design. Newcomers are attending workshops, reading books, or listening to podcasts and walking away with an inkling of a concept that seems easy to understand. There is caché in being "design aware". Yet when these people come face to face with an actual design challenge, they discover there are unforeseen consequences to their high-minded concepts and sticky notes.

Design in legal is powerful and potent

The growing cadre of design newcomers in legal is an amazing development. While there are risks and challenges, they are worth experiencing as the potential for applying design methods in legal is immense. Both design thinking and design provide a unique combination of skills, perspective, tools, and behaviors that have a significant likelihood of unlocking constraints to make real things happen. But to succeed, the design community in legal must recognize and own both its limitations and its responsibilities. It must mature along the three core capabilities of measurement, insight, and execution. While these familiar words are commonly understood in most businesses, design expands them to include new methods of use and application. This ability to expand use and generate value from doing so is the real challenge facing design in legal.

Measurement

This is the ability to capture data and information relating to activities and behaviors within the organization itself as well as by external actors like buyers and competitors in the marketplace. What is measured, what can be measured, and what should be measured inside most firms is rarely examined. Many tend to think measurement only pertains to accounting and financial systems. While the general practice in legal is to measure only rudimentary things such as revenue, hours, overhead costs, realization, and profits, there is a vast array of other metrics that can be employed across the firm or in pockets of it.

Example:
Resource validation – exploring the organization and identifying all resources that include talent, capabilities, technology, processes, and even culture. Once identified, each would be measured based on its:

- Accessibility – is it available and are processes in place to use it?
- Condition – how well does it work or how willing is it to work?
- Value – what value does the resource currently create and what is its potential?
- Rarity – is the resource commonly found in the organization or market or is it truly unique?
- Ability to imitate and replicate – how easy is it to get more of these resources?
- Organized – how well is the resource utilized within the organization? Is it a stand-alone asset or is it fully integrated into a system or work structure?

Insight

This is the ability to interpret data and information into meaningful analysis that raises and answers relevant questions about the firm and its competitive options. The ability to generate useful insights intentionally and consistently goes far beyond the mechanics of producing reports, spreadsheets, and lists on an established cadence. The power of insight is that it provides context; a unique vantage point of key realities and strategic options that is based on the specifics of the firm's current operational and competitive performance. Insight also surfaces opportunities that the organization can and should address through concrete decisions and actions. It informs leaders on not just what is happening but on what might or can happen, providing them with greater clarity and validity on potential decisions.

Example:
Workflow mapping is a visual depiction of the sequence of steps that it takes to produce an output. It defines tasks and identifies the resources used, tools/capabilities applied, and time spent. These can be applied to both operational processes like the conflicts process as well as legal work product like litigation or transactions.

The user journey is a visual representation of how a "user" actually experiences a process or interaction. A user can be a customer or client, a lawyer doing legal work, an employee taking care of business, or some other human who is involved. It seeks to identify each touchpoint or interaction a human has with the overall process. Touchpoints can be positive, negative, or neutral. There is an immense amount of insight gained from this method as "experience" is one of the most overlooked yet most vital components of design success.

Execution

By execution, we mean the ability to deliver an outcome or stimulate new activity or behaviors within the organization. Because business-side talent directly controls or influences many of the firm's operational and performance levers, many business and law professionals have a real ability to take action and drive execution across a number of areas. The core resources and data needed for measurement and insight are either immediately accessible or fairly easy to acquire for business talent. Once developed, these new capabilities must spur some type of action or create an impact within the firm. The ability to execute requires a certain mindset and set of skills that can be developed through preparation and practice.

Examples:

Validity

Is the idea solving a problem that your organization and target market even recognize? Will the organization support the advancement of the idea and how easy is it to communicate its value?

A valid option encompasses solutions and language that firm leadership and partners find cogent, coherent, and most of all, applicable and relevant to the firm and its current position and ambitions. Also, validity speaks to the defensibility of the process used to define and shape the option. This is in addition to, but should not be confused with, "viability", which is often referenced as a design parameter but measures sustainability of the idea.

Feasibility

What will it take to gain support for, actually build, and maintain this option? A feasible option consumes resources as efficiently and effectively as possible, given current availability/scarcity, while achieving maximum value. It does this in a timeline that paces ahead of hostile efforts or ambivalent forces that will impede progress. Also, feasibility addresses such intangibles as political resistance, change management, and resource availability.

Desirability

What will the level of interest be from external parties (clients, competitors, media, etc.) and internal parties (fee earners, leadership, business talent) and will they want to participate/learn more? A desirable option attracts curiosity and builds momentum for further development on the part of leadership and the firm generally. If the idea's value is too murky, difficult to communicate and convey, or appears incomplete, it will suffer from erosion of support and emotional commitment.

Accelerating maturity

So, the answer is no, legal design is not bullsh*t. It is simply new and emerging within legal and is enjoying a surging enthusiasm among newcomers who are trying to learn the craft but only have limited exposure to it. Design has proven highly effective outside of legal and there are already strong successes within legal – from access to justice efforts to new business creation in the BigLaw market.

Its focus on the user, the client, the customer – in essence, the human – is key to its success. Not only does this mindset generate creative and highly valuable insight into how to address problems and opportunities, it also helps address the change management burden.

In essence, humans drive acceptance and adoption because they have to use or interact with any new change. They can ignore it, screw it up, use it differently than intended, or seek to undermine it. And this happens a lot. The "not invented here" syndrome of organizational R&D efforts is a perfect example of this. This holds true for lawyers especially. Often, I have seen lawyers thumb their noses at a new successful campaign, service, or project simply because they were not part of the process or do not understand the process used to achieve success. It is infuriating for anyone who experiences this response, but this is part of the learning and the job of design. This highlights the importance of not just generating new ideas but making sure they can and will be actually used and adopted. That is the really tough design challenge.

Design is about one thing and one thing only. It is about creating measurable value. To succeed as a commonly accepted capability, design must be directly correlated to business strategy. It must suppress jargon and emphasize action. Its value should not be measured based on events like jam sessions, whiteboard brainstorming, post-it notes, sketches, or doodling. Its value must be demonstrated in an evidence-based manner. It must use metrics that an organization will recognize and respect. Often the designer must introduce new metrics, explain and defend them, and then foster adoption. The designer must account for change management and design for culture, systems, business and operations practices, and politics. The bulk of work for a business or service designer is crafting integration and adoption. Without that, they fail. Regardless of how brilliant the idea. Regardless of the process used to generate it. If a business rejects or is unable to adopt the solution, the designer has failed.

We cannot allow design to fail in legal. It is too important, legal that is. The services lawyers provide are often hidden in our society and economy. Few look forward to calling their lawyer, finding a lawyer, or even talking to a lawyer. It is not a user-friendly domain – for individuals or organizations. Law firms are typically not easy to do business with. Neither are many in-house teams, as their internal business customers will share. As designers, we owe it to clients of all types to take design seriously, tap into its unique approach to unlock and uncover unmet needs. Once accomplished, we can build robust businesses and services around addressing these needs. When you build something people actually want instead of begrudgingly need, it gets easier. Make no mistake, it will take work, hard work, but so worth the effort.

Chapter 8:

Learning to see – crafting insights for new services

By Lann Wasson, associate director of legal project management, Husch Blackwell

Every day the legal industry is inundated with announcements about innovative solutions. From all sides of the market, organizations are pursuing new ways to deliver services, creating products from existing expertise, and testing the viability of new business models. The overarching emphasis on technology solutions sometimes leads to the misconception that to be "innovative" one must use the latest tools, especially artificial intelligence. This was the case in a client session earlier this year when a team from Husch Blackwell was invited to participate in discussions about how the legal department could innovate like other areas within the company. In the rush to adopt technology, many organizations lose sight of their customers, their needs, and the way their customers experience their services.

As a human-centered approach to innovation, design thinking starts with the customer and includes a number of approaches and techniques to uncover latent needs and develop insights, which can ultimately lead to new solutions, technology or otherwise, that delight customers. Empathize, the centerpiece of the model, plays an important role in all phases of innovation by keeping the voice of the customer in the room. To develop greater empathy for our customers, legal professionals need to cultivate a mindset of curiosity in order to see each customer's situation and needs from the customer's perspective. With the growing emphasis on the client experience as a way to differentiate services, developing skills to understand the customer perspective is becoming critical to demonstrating value.

In a legal setting, learning to see the customer's perspective is often a matter of learning to listen for context clues. By discussing observations and crafting insights from site visits, interviews, client meetings, interactions at conferences and conversations over coffee, among other activities, individual lawyers and other professionals working as a team can learn why a customer cares about an issue and how a provider can serve them best going forward. Changing the perception of the problem and including the emotional dimension is also a great way to motivate a team to approach an issue more creatively. It's natural for people to respond to their world in creative ways, so to learn more about what people are trying to accomplish, legal professionals need to develop more expertise in understanding people.

At Husch Blackwell we focus on four areas within the design thinking toolkit to help teams learn to see problems from their customer's perspective – practice observing, learning from extremes, conducting interviews, and crafting insights. While these techniques are fairly straightforward, performing them well with empathy takes practice. To increase the number of opportunities to experiment with design techniques, we also encourage people to exercise their creative muscles in their daily work and life. Getting outside of one's familiar environment is one of the best ways to practice these techniques, whether that involves visiting a local art museum, taking a walk on a trail by a nearby university or engaging in a new activity.

Practice observing

A good place to start learning about the things people care about and what they value is to use your eyes and ears to cultivate a mindset of curiosity. While there are plenty of opportunities to practice observation techniques throughout the day, developing one's capabilities requires a degree of intentionality. For instance, if you are invited to visit with someone in their office, look for the themes represented by the artifacts in their workspace. Are they a sports fan, do they volunteer or serve on a board, or is their family front and center? Ask yourself, what does this person value? Based on my observations, if I could ask this person one question to get to know them better, what would it be?

To practice observing the values of a company, take note of the way a client organization presents itself when you walk into their main lobby. If they have recently renovated their space, what do those changes signal about what the company values? Ask yourself, how do representatives of the company greet me when I enter? How do people interact with each other? If you are spending the day visiting a facility, ask people to talk about why they perform activities the way they do. Listen closely to the language they use as it often reveals something about what the company values. Or during your commute to work, find a restaurant or coffee shop and observe the way the business operates and changes over time.

Ask those in management as well as employees on the floor why the company implemented those changes.

Sometimes it's helpful to think of the activity as a movie versus a snapshot. For example, if you are listening to a conference call with a number of participants in the room, a panel discussion on a topic, or even participating in a happy hour event in the office, ask yourself how is this conversation unfolding? Why is it going in this direction? Who is setting the tone or framing the discussion? Depending on a person's social media or online profile, one can conduct a similar exercise by looking at someone's posts, pictures, or tweets. For social content ask yourself the same series of questions about themes, what someone values, and what would you like to know more about. While it's possible to practice some of these techniques online, the best way to observe people is in context, to see them interact with their spaces and the other people around them.

At Husch Blackwell we have studied what designers at innovation labs look for when they are conducting design projects. Typically, they keep six things in mind when observing their subjects. First, design researchers look for things that prompt behavior, such as a sign, a sound, or something that triggers an event. Second, they look for adaptions, the things people do to work around an issue to make their experience better. For instance, if you are learning about the way new associates use time entry software, you could watch what they do when they get stuck or if the software loads slowly. Third, experienced designers look for what people care about, because this is often a window into what they value.

Fourth, they look for body language as a cue to someone's emotions. Identifying body language that is in contrast to what is being said is often an indication that someone needs something. In one of our attorney interviews for a recent design session, one lawyer's facial expression conveyed that they were uncomfortable answering a question, which led to an insight about some of the needs of their group. Fifth, design professionals look for patterns or recurring themes as these also reveal what people value. And, sixth they look for the unexpected – what might seem out of place in the context of the broader environment.

Learn from extremes

Extreme perspectives can stretch the way you think about a problem and help you discover your underlying assumptions. Looking at extremes can also be a source of inspiration because extreme users often illustrate the same needs and desires of the rest of a group. For example, during a number of Husch Blackwell's shark-tank style competitions, we looked at the differences in the way new associates and seasoned partners pitched their ideas and then compared their approaches to pitches made using the business model canvas framework. In a legal setting, extreme users can be found within one's own organization as well as in other areas of the industry, such as at start-ups, solo-practitioners, colleagues in co-working spaces, remote workers, former in-house or law firm peers or virtual networks.

Sometimes it's helpful to identify extreme users in analogous situations, especially if they are more accessible for observation and interviews. For example, as a cyclist I have observed that people who are just starting out riding with a group are often intimidated by the more experienced riders and all of the specialist gear in a bicycle shop. To gain empathy for these individuals, I put myself in a situation of buying supplies at a beauty store to understand more deeply what it felt like again to be in a new and unfamiliar situation. Analogous situations are sometimes hard to identify outside of one's industry, unless you look for scenarios with similar kinds of tasks. A colleague and I will sometimes take peers from other industries out to lunch just to learn more about their daily life in their organizations and look for connections, patterns, and insights into our own work.

When looking at extremes it is important to strike a balance among the different kinds of outliers, so that one extreme doesn't over-inform the discussion. The various lenses for extremes often include demographic attributes such as age, gender, and ethnicity, different kinds of behavior or levels of experience, attitudes about a topic, familiarity with a product or service, life stage or motivations. When picking a lens it is important to be specific about the persona. For instance, is a novice a first year associate, an associate general counsel new to the role, a newly minted legal operations director or someone who is using a new software tool for the first time? Is an expert a partner at a law firm, a seasoned general counsel, a data scientist, or a recent lateral hire? Once you have decided on the lens that is most relevant to the topic, try to identify five or six potential extremes and stretch yourself beyond the most obvious attributes.

Interviews

Conducting a great interview is more than asking a series of great questions, although investing time in crafting the right questions is essential to having a meaningful conversation. Setting the stage by building rapport and paying close attention to your own non-verbal cues, such as your posture, eye contact and facial expressions, demonstrates empathy and curiosity. By deepening the connection with the person you are interviewing, you facilitate a more comfortable and candid conversation, often leading to deeper insights. Pacing also makes a difference in the quality of the interview as you move from building rapport to your first topics of interest. Sometimes an interviewee will need time to reflect on their answer, so it's important not to fill the silence or make them feel rushed.

Open-ended questions allow the interviewee to share examples of a time when something occurred. They also allow the interviewer to ask why, with genuine curiosity, and uncover more of the situation as seen by the person and their rationale. For instance, during one of our P3 interviews, in response to a why question, one of our partners shared a need to integrate her team more closely with other real estate lawyers to help them become more adept at looking at the client's situation more creatively. Along these lines it is also important not to insert yourself into the conversation, to avoid being defensive or testing the interviewee for the "right" answer.

Sometimes what the interviewee says doesn't match their body language and this situation creates an opportunity to ask about what wasn't said. In many of our legal project management workshops, our team simulates an interview with a general counsel. Since lawyers usually jump right into the substantive discussion, debriefing the simulation highlights open-ended questions that could have been asked about the fictional GC, their background, tenure at the company, how they report up in the organization, etc. Conducting focused interviews with open-ended questions takes practice and patience, but leads to the kind of conversation that reveals insights.

At Husch Blackwell, one of the ways we bring the voice of the customer to a team is to record interviews with a number of stakeholders who hold different customer perspectives or perform different roles. For instance, on a design project with the firm's pricing team, we interviewed client relationship managers from a number of industry teams who had different levels of pricing confidence. Then, we asked the pricing team members to individually write down "How Might We…?" questions as they listened to the interviews as a group. This allowed the whole team to hear what was being said, watch the person's body language and listen for and discern their needs. After posting hundreds of notes up on white-boards, the team began to see several themes emerge and understand through voting techniques which topics resonated with the whole group.

Crafting insights

In many cases outside of a design context, individual observations remain locked away in the mind of the person or at best are shared in a meeting without making the kinds of connections that lead to real insights. For observations to become an insight, they should be authentic, non-obvious, and reveal something about the way someone thought or felt. Often, design teams will look for interesting stories or interactions among stakeholders, something unexpected, or something that revealed someone's motivations or frustrations. For example, after one listening session with a corporate law department on the topic of legal operations, a team from Husch Blackwell uncovered a need to deliver content to the associate general counsel in a format that she could share directly with those she reported to. Sometimes, interpreting observations requires reading between the lines to sort out the gaps between what was said, someone's body language, and possibly their workaround.

Working as a team, participants in a design session can create themes from patterns of observations and write headlines that describe the best stories for each category. This is often an iterative process to find the right connections and most significant observations. Like the process of finding patterns in the stars to create constellations, and then telling the story of their formation, crafting insights as a team is challenging, but the collaboration can lead to statements that are more informative, inspiring, and memorable. If the team is composed of individuals from a number of disciplines, sometimes they will find gaps or connections between their disciplines that form the basis for new service ideas. Ultimately, the objective of an insight is to motivate the team towards solutions, so it is important not to rush the process and find the most compelling insights.

Crafting insights also requires a shift in the way information is delivered today. Instead of going around the room in a team meeting and sharing an update, teams should consider developing other kinds of deliverables, such as a portfolio piece, insights report, or design brief, to motivate the individual stakeholders. For example, one of Husch Blackwell's design briefs for a lateral hiring project included a timeline with some direct quotations from lateral interviews about key moments in their journey to the firm. This allowed the team to highlight an aspect of lateral hiring that is sometimes overlooked, as some laterals have a long runway into the firm and require a greater degree of engagement overtime to bring them on board. Mapping the journey and focusing on the key moments where that engagement would make the most difference was a key insight for this project.

The techniques of design thinking hold promise for those in the legal industry interested in understanding their customers' needs and providing a better overall client experience. Although challenging at times, working as a team will create buy-in and motivate people to think more creatively about possible solutions. At Husch Blackwell we have found that keeping the customer's voice in the room through observation techniques, looking at extremes, interviews, and crafting memorable insights can also lead to new ideas for products and services.

Chapter 9: Legal design psych-ops jujitsu

By Tess Blair, litigator and legal entrepreneur, Morgan, Lewis & Bockius LLP

The case for legal design

We have all experienced bad design. In his classic book, *The Design of Everyday Things*,[1] Don Norman assures us that it's not you, it's bad design, when you push on a pull door and then smile sheepishly after smashing your face into the glass. Or when you press a walk button at an intersection and then stand obediently while nothing happens. Have you tried to navigate a website but accidently closed the tab? You are not (necessarily) a Luddite – that's bad design.

We have all experienced good design too. But, like a well-behaved toddler, good design rarely gets noticed. And that's because good design just works. It does what it was intended to do and the user intuitively knows how to use it. That isn't by accident; that's by design. Successful businesses have long known the impact that design can have on sales and customer service. According to the Design Management Institute, design-focused companies like Apple, Ford, Starbucks, Target, and Nike outperform the S&P 500 by over 200 percent.[2] These companies outperform their peers by a two-to-one margin. And McKinsey, in its comprehensive study "The Business Value of Design", found a strong correlation between design focus and financial performance.[3] Those businesses scoring highest on the McKinsey design focus measure increased revenues and shareholder value more than their peers over a five-year period – 32 percent higher revenue growth and 56 percent greater increase in shareholder value. This is true across industries, whether the company's products are physical things, digital products, services, or a combination of these. So, we can all agree that good design doesn't just save us from embarrassment like a properly designed door, and it isn't just cool like a Jony Ive-designed iPhone (although it is both of those things). Good design is good business.

But what is design and, more to the point, what is legal design? At its essence, design is creative problem-solving. And *good* design is creative problem-solving that focuses on improving the user's experience with the thing. Legal design is not legal problem-solving per se – that's called the practice of law. Instead, legal design is legal service delivery design or, as we call it in our eData practice group, client experience design. Client experience design examines the ways that clients interact with and consume the legal information and advice they get from us. Our aim is to improve that experience.

What does bad legal design look like? How about good legal design? What if the current state of legal design is, at best, neither good nor bad because most legal service delivery is un-designed?[4] Hear me out on this – legal design is a new phenomenon. Law firms, legal departments, and legal service providers (more the latter than the others) have only recently embraced legal design as a means to obtain a competitive advantage in the same way they earlier embraced process improvement methods like Legal Lean Sigma[5] and legal project management to drive efficiency, reduce cost, and offer the amorphous "added value". All of these business methods are of a piece, and all began to get a foothold in legal following last decade's financial crisis.

No longer cloaked in budgetary autonomy, legal departments began over the last decade to slowly and systematically apply business management principles to the purchase and control of legal services.[6] Lessons learned from the commoditization of eDiscovery also began to find purchase well upstream of document review. Disaggregation and the increased competition it wrought in eDiscovery brought labor arbitrage, process improvement, and specialized legal technology to the profession. Big (law firm spend) data, transparency, alternative fee agreements, legal project management, innovation, and design thinking have gotten traction, becoming the cost of entry for some clients who ask us to help them deliver better, faster, cheaper, and more valuable results for their legal spend.

Design thinking may be new to legal, but it isn't new to our clients. The smartest businesses have long used these techniques in every aspect of their business, from R&D to marketing. And so it should surprise no one that design has made its way to legal. As any student of the profession quickly observes, improvements in the delivery of legal services, like many changes in the profession, are predominantly client driven. Further fueling adoption of legal design is the stark reality[7] the legal profession will face when the next recession inevitably comes. Article after study after article portends the end of BigLaw at the hands of its emulators. The list of purported causes is long but instructive[8] – lagging legal productivity, client (dis)satisfaction, increased competition for core legal services from the Big Four and alternative legal service providers, automation and legal tech, economic uncertainty, and deregulation of the bar.[9] I would add another – increased competition for stagnant legal spend from our own clients, whose legal departments are growing in size and diversity of talent and handling more of the legal work themselves.

Because legal service delivery is the way we deliver legal services to *clients*, it only makes sense then that good legal design is client-centered.[10] To ensure that it is, we make the client the anchor of our legal design process. Before every Legal Design Jam at Morgan Lewis, we start by asking, "What is this like for the client? How might we improve the way our client interacts with...? How would this client prefer to consume legal content? How can we present this information in a way that makes it useful to this client?" To gather this information we, ahem, ask the client.[11]

But I'm getting ahead of myself. What, exactly, is a Legal Design Jam?

Introducing the Legal Design Jam

Great lawyers and legal design are like oil and water – the very things that make great lawyers so great makes them less than amenable to the legal design process. The design process requires the designer to be comfortable with vulnerability. Good lawyers just aren't. We lawyers don't like to fail. We don't want to share (feelings, not stuff). We avoid criticism. So, *how* do we convince lawyers to participate in a design process that requires sharing, creativity, and (dramatic pause) failure?

At Morgan Lewis, our answer is the Legal Design Jam. This exercise – structured as a shark-tank style competition – teaches lawyers how to get out of their own way so they can engage with the design process. To learn how it works, let's dive into its component parts, starting with the people who make up a legal design team.

The legal design team

The legal design team is where the magic either happens, or it doesn't. That, in turn, depends on how well the team works together toward the collective goal. Some ground rules and/or helpful suggestions underpin how we do it at Morgan Lewis:

Overall, the team should be a minimum of five people and a maximum of about ten. You need enough people to create a diverse set of perspectives but not so many that people can fade into the background. Ideally, the client is represented on the team and can even be half of the team or more. After all, the lawyers know the law and the clients know the problem, and you want to have both of those perspectives in the room and at the table.

Try to include paralegals, secretaries, partners, associates, IT professionals, business managers, and so on. We strive to include people with unique viewpoints because team diversity is critical, and not just in the demographic capital-D Diversity sense. That is super important and mission critical, but I also mean diversity of work experiences, education levels, culture, background, and life experience. We stage the Jam to ensure participation from each member of the team, which can be tricky with lawyers on the team. While lawyers always agree to share the mic in principle, some find it hard in execution. We lawyers are all about meritocracy when we're sitting on top of the pile, and we know intellectually that intellectual diversity is critically important to innovation, but most of us still think we have the best ideas. (We don't.) And we need to stop talking and try listening instead. (We can't.)

A Design Jam is timed, by the way, so our design management team has their work cut out for them. Good lawyers like to "work the ref" and tend to see things like rules and timers as merely aspirational. Thus, each team (or group of teams depending on how many you are lucky to have available) should also include a design lead and a project manager to facilitate the Jam and keep the design process (and lawyers) on track. The designer is usually a member of my eData team but usually doesn't play a major role in the actual design and development process. The project manager functions as the referee and may be from my team or from the client or another practice or business area altogether. A good project manager and great referee should be proactive and optimistic, have a bottomless sense of humor, and be a good communicator. They should also be very good at identifying systemic problems rather than focusing on the "symptoms" of those problems (forest v. trees). Oh, and a high tolerance for stress is key. Good lawyers are stressful.[12]

Can teams have a personality? No, but the most successful design teams behave in a certain way. They are enthusiastic. They cheer and encourage one another. Rather than judging ideas of others, they build on them with a "That is so great, we could take that idea and add this..." They are collectively patient, knowing that design is a process and letting that process work, enjoying it even, and are willing to explore lots of zany ideas that will never become things because the right idea will inevitably emerge. They are also empathetic, able to understand the problem to be solved from the perspective of the client and willing to share theirs. The successful team is willing to fail forward, knowing that the learning and the improvement of an idea comes from not quite nailing it and finding out why. And, of course, a great team is collaborative and egalitarian, with an open mic where everybody shares because there are no bad ideas. This is what we strive to create. A happy, patient, zany, compassionate, enthusiastic, vulnerable team, making work play. Sounds like a utopia, right? Uh, not so fast. This, in a nutshell, is a HUGE problem for legal design. I mean, those aren't exactly the traits that come to mind when you think of successful lawyers, are they?

Traits of successful lawyers

Lawyers are special people, and if you use the term "non-lawyer" to describe everybody else in the building and you're a lawyer, well, you're very special.[13] Here's the problem – the very things it takes to be a successful lawyer are pretty much the exact opposite of what it takes to be successful in design thinking. This isn't my opinion. It's science.

According to research from Dr Larry Richard[14] successful lawyers have the following dominant personality traits (the numbers in parentheses indicate the strength of these traits, compared to a base value of 50 percent for the average person who isn't a lawyer):

- Skepticism (90);
- Autonomy (89);
- Abstract reasoning (82);
- Urgency (71);
- Resilience (30); and
- Sociability (7).

Lawyers come by some of these traits naturally, while others are trained into them in law school and during the practice of law itself. We're taught to question everything – that's how we identify legal problems, spot loopholes, and pinpoint issues for argument. We trust our own judgment and hone an ability to think on our feet, which makes us generally reluctant to follow other people's instructions or rely on ideas or goals that we didn't set ourselves. We're in the habit of thinking critically about situations and pointing out conflicting ideas, a habit we can't necessarily suppress in other settings.[15] We're quintessentially impatient, always in a rush, in love with efficiency, and intolerant of wasting time. We have a low tolerance for criticism and we are terrified of failure, which leads us to avoid situations and activities where we might be rejected or we might "lose". And we're not terribly interested in making new personal connections or sharing our inner lives with other people, especially when it comes to touchy-feely stuff like feelings or emotions. No thank you![16]

As you can surmise, these traits are problematic for legal design, which needs people on design teams to be optimistic, collaborative, capable of concrete reasoning, patient, resilient (failure-tolerant), and social – the exact opposite of successful lawyers.

But why? Why does legal design require all of this kumbaya stuff that gives most lawyers a rash? Why can't we skip all that and Just. Fix. The. Problem. [Insert primal lawyer scream here.] Let's look at how design actually works to understand why these traits are so critical to good design.

The legal design process

The Legal Design Jam is an abbreviated version of the legal design process itself. There are five steps in legal design (or, really, any design thinking or human-centered design process).

1. Empathize

You can't design anything until you know who you're designing for. Who is the user? What matters to them? What's important? Learn about your audience through both observation and interviews. Maybe you think you already know – but you should still ask.

What does your customer's journey look like? How do they engage with you, and how do they feel about each of those touchpoints? What do they love, and what are they not all that happy about? How could you transform their reaction from "meh" to absolute delight? Don't guess; ask.

2. Define

What does this user need from you right now? How can you narrow down the problem they're having into something discrete and solvable?

3. Ideate

Brainstorm time! Come up with as many creative solutions as possible to your defined problem. Wild ideas are strongly encouraged. *Judging is not allowed.* Yes, lawyers, I'm talking to you! There are no bad ideas in a brainstorming session. The goal is to come up with as many possible solutions as you can. Impossible ideas? Bring them on. Zany ideas? Let's hear them. Ideas that no one could ever afford in a million years? Who cares; you're not paying for it. Stuff the judgment and let the ideas flow.

4. Prototype

Pick one or more of your ideas and build a physical representation of it that you can show to others. How can you illustrate or depict your idea?

Remember: this prototype is just a rough draft. It does not need to be perfect (in fact, it shouldn't be).

What do prototypes look like? Your prototype might be:

- A storyboard with different scenes depicting a solution;
- A few simple screenshots showing how a user would engage with the solution;
- A moodboard or vision board;
- A 3D model;
- A structure assembled with blocks;
- A sketch of a wireframe;
- A cardboard 2D model;
- A Kanban-like board with sticky notes showing a process;
- An advertisement for the final product;
- A mound of Play-Doh you mindlessly stabbed with your pen while judging sotto voce everyone else's ideas (don't do this one. I am just making sure you are paying attention); and/or
- A drawing on paper or a whiteboard.

Your imagination is really the only limit when it comes to depicting your solution.

5. Test

Rate your prototypes. Which are most likely to solve the user's problem or result in a significant improvement? Which are most likely to make your audience happy? Which are most likely to disrupt an established field? (Hint: the answer is not always "mine".)

Now, share your prototyped idea or ideas with your original audience and get some feedback (it won't kill you). What worked? What didn't? What needs to be tweaked? Do you need to start all over? When the client said they need something to "move forward", did you go Ferrari while she went bus token? Eliminate any ideas that don't work and identify ways to make your good ideas better. Figure out the specifications for your ultimate solution – what will it cost and how long will it take to build?

Boom. You've just done a round of legal design. Now, let's look at what it takes for the process to really come to life – especially once you add lawyers, with all of their specialness, to the mix.

Making legal design work in an inhospitable clime

As a trained designer and lawyer who has had the opportunity to work with and observe lawyers in their natural habitat for two decades, I can think of no place less hospitable to creativity, playful ideation, and egalitarian problem-solving than a law firm. I say that with great affection and respect for my colleagues and peers (no, really). That does not mean that attempting legal design in law is futile. To the contrary, with so much potential for improvement and a market wide open to competition, design in law is imperative. So, the greatest value of our Legal Design Jam may very well be the techniques we use to reduce this embedded resistance to the creative process.

The techniques we have developed to do this fall into three categories – optimizing the design team, proactively boosting the team's engagement, and then my personal favorite, using what I call psych-ops jujitsu to rewire the lawyers (even if only temporarily) to relax, think creatively, work collaboratively, and even – gasp! – fail productively. Let's take a closer look at each of these concepts.

Optimize your team

Teams have to be both diverse and empowered to be truly successful. I'll repeat that. Teams have to be both diverse and empowered to be truly successful. Got it?

Diversity is critical to innovation and should include as many kinds of intellectual, experiential, and demographic diversity as you can cram into the team. It includes diversity of skill and experience as well as general style and approach toward life. A diverse design team should include optimists and pessimists, millennials and Gen Xers, city dwellers and country folk, vegans and carnivores, right brains, left brains, math people [insert lawyer joke here], and so on. A good legal design team, in particular, has lawyers, sure, but it also has paralegals and, if we're lucky, secretaries, receptionists, IT, HR, and other lawyer-adjacent and business roles. It has people who are serious (again, the lawyers) as well as more lighthearted people who will bring humor into the process. It might have a partner, but it really needs a few associates to balance those experience levels.

For diversity to have any meaning and impact on design, every member of the team must be empowered and freed to participate without hesitation. We have developed a few tools to ensure that everyone at the table – from the senior partner to the recently hired file clerk – feels empowered to share and contribute. First, middle, and last, we need to shut the lawyers up every once in a while and let everyone else talk!

To do that, we use an "open mic" setup where everyone has a voice and every voice is heard and valued.

We also emphasize that we're a judgment-free zone, and we lay those ground rules out as many times and in as many ways as we need to drive that point home. This is especially important in brainstorming – judgment is kryptonite when it comes to creative ideation. But come on – sometimes people bring up bad ideas, right? Or ideas that are totally out of place for what the team is trying to accomplish! Are we supposed to just go with the flow and cheer for those crappy ideas? Yes, yes we are. Every idea has value, even if that value is simply giving the next person a jolt of inspiration that leads to another idea. IDEO is great at this (along with everything else they do there).[17]

To enforce the judgment-free zone in a non-punitive way, we use a technique called the "parking lot".[18] If someone throws in an idea that doesn't fit for where we are, we park it in the parking lot. (It's usually a big piece of paper stuck on the wall and labeled – wait for it – "parking lot".) We do not dismiss it, particularly if it is an idea we want to return to later. For example, if we are brainstorming ways to solve a communication problem, ideas like homing pigeon, post-its, wikis, sign language, color coding, etc. may start flying. Then, when a participant (probably a lawyer) throws out, "There's an iPhone app for that. Done. Can I leave now?" we may note that in the parking lot in case we ultimately decide that a technical/software-based solution is the right way to go.

Finally, we encourage constructive failure. That is, we find ways to find something positive from any failure by learning from it. Sure, an idea may not work, but here's why – and here's the good nugget at the center that we *can* use.

Boost engagement

To boost engagement, we focus on raising everyone's positive emotions by inspiring them, relaxing them, and warming them up for creative thinking. One of the most fascinating things I learned from Dr Richard is that there is a physical, biochemical explanation to a lot of this stuff. Turns out that our obstinance (or what I call PITA Syndrome) is wired into our autonomic nervous system. Our training and our work as lawyers hardwires us for stress. We are by nature and training skeptical, suspicious, and dubious. We are paid to find the problems, not the rainbows. This perpetual negativity machine inhabiting our skulls makes our bodies churn out cortisol and adrenaline like a Pez dispenser. These stress hormones trigger a fight-or-flight reflex that includes high blood pressure, pupil dilation, and dry mouth. While that look sounds absolutely charming, our aim in staging a legal design program is to short-circuit that stuff and get a few lawyers to chill.

Play is a big, huge, massive part of the process for that very reason. That's why I always have Play-Doh or other toys in my brainstorming box (more about those boxes in a minute). Any guess what happens when we play? Our bodies release endorphins. Yum. Endorphins are "feel good" hormones that reduce stress, increase your sense of wellbeing, stimulate your creativity, and, IMHO, make you a nicer human in general. And that is actually charming.[19]

To decrease cortisol (boo) and increase endorphins (yay), we also focus on creating an environment conducive to relaxation. Not the kind that makes you drool and doze off, but the kind that inspires and secures. Nature, great views, color, texture, and light all impact our senses and our brains. The trick is conjuring an environment that inspires but does not stress. I mean, you're not getting yelled at for a mediocre idea if everyone's feeling Zen, are you?[20]

We have a few tools to get everyone feeling (calmly, serenely) inspired. First, we give some thought to the environment. I never want to work in a dark or windowless room. Spare me the PowerPoint (please!). Natural settings are great; a few picnic tables under a tree would be terrific. We'll often inspire the team by pointing out a few analogous acts of excellence. Think of Jony Ive and Steve Jobs, people who have really taken creative design to a whole new level. We're also sure to inject and encourage both humor and joyfulness. Humor is great, with a major caveat – it should never be at someone's expense (not even your own) or you might as well jolt everyone with a hit of cortisol. It causes stress. Instead, we try to create an environment that encourages joy, because joy is incompatible with criticism.[21]

Think that's too frou-frou and wouldn't possibly work on our big legal brains? Lawyers, I hate to tell you, but you're pretty easy to manipulate. Lawyers love to hear that they're awesome (well, ok, everybody loves to hear that they're awesome), but praise like that really sets up a positive atmosphere – one that lowers everyone's cortisol and encourages the team to relax and play.

We also raise positive emotions by incentivizing our groups. The chief incentive is the fact that the Legal Design Jam exercise is a *competition*. That means that there is a prize, and there is a winner. We love winning. One important side note here – the prize cannot be money. While everybody loves winning, putting real money on the table will totally backfire by increasing everyone's stress levels (damned cortisol!). Instead, the prize is recognition, praise, and attention. We also praise people for speaking up.

This sounds like Dog Training 101, and not a thing that would work with sophisticated lawyers and business people, but we really are Pavlovian when it comes to praise and other positive recognition.[22] Real, sincere praise, recognition, and/or cookies work. Now, who's a good boy?

Use psych-ops jujitsu

Now for my favorite part. We use a few specific psychological maneuvers to get our lawyers to want to really engage in our design process. We counter the "anti-designer" and we (try to) make the process irresistible.

Great lawyers are, by default, "anti-designers". So to engage them in the legal design process, we need to break down those barriers that make them so reluctant to engage by showing the way and rewarding (any glimpse of) creative behavior. This all sounds like rubbish, so let me provide some actionable steps that work. Share examples of successful design. Relate the legal design process to the practice of law and talk about a successful colleague's "out-of-the-box" thinking that made her a successful rainmaker. Use storytelling to draw a picture of a well-designed legal solution and a happy client's thrill. Have a design lead at the table to role model good creative behavior, even if they have to exaggerate their schtick to encourage lawyers to engage even a little.

We also practice creative resilience, we destigmatize failure, and use a technique called systematic inventive thinking.[23] This is a genius way to get lawyers to engage in creative work. With systematic inventive thinking, we create safety by the way we structure the design project. We don't say, "Here's the client's problem, now go solve it". Instead, we define the problem just enough in advance in a way that eliminates the team's need to debate the problem and enables the team to focus on solutions instead. We may also use this technique during ideation exercises, by limiting possible solutions. We may ask: "How would you solve this problem if you had only $5?" "What would you do if you could not use technology to solve it?" This won't reduce fear of failure to zero. But by defining the problem to be solved and limiting options, we are eliminating the paralysis that can come from endless possibilities or too many choices (i.e., the blank page, 31 flavors, 57 channels).[24] In a Design Jam, team members freezing up and keeling over like frightened goats (google it) is not a good look. So we aim to eliminate the possibility of fear paralysis where we can and by creating these conditions of safety, the team may relax enough to be creative.

Getting lawyers over their fear of failure is a major hurdle that requires us to confront some long-established habits and some of that internal plumbing that has hardwired the most successful lawyers to avoid risk.

Remember how you shook things up when you were a kid? That's right – you went to camp.

Fail camp

Fail camp is a quick exercise we use to teach teams to fail better – and to *like it*.[25] Fail camp serves two purposes. First, it desensitizes our lawyers to failure in a safe environment. They just get used to it, and it stings less each time. Practicing failure also shows everyone that failure is okay. Without getting too meta here, failure doesn't mean we are flawed or broken people; failure makes us human and failure is simply part of the process (of living and of designing). Second, we can start teaching teams to use failure to their advantage. (jujitsu anyone?) Each time you try and fail, you get closer to success. You are learning and improving the service or the process that you strive to build, which you cannot really do well without meaningful feedback. If we have the time, we workshop with our sponsors and clients on how to provide constructive, helpful feedback for design teams. Most of the time, in the heat of a design jam, we coach through the process to show everyone how to deliver feedback in a constructive way. Less sting, more zing.

We encourage teams to fail fast, fail often, and fail safely, and we reward truly epic fails. That's right, we make failure fun. And we make failure part of the process and a competition teams can win. (Jujitsu again!) We use that competitive nature to make our teams actually *want* to fail. For example, we relieve the stress of trying to find the best answer by challenging our teams to find the worst solution. What would really stink for the client? What would be outrageously expensive and inefficient? We get them thinking about opposites, inverting questions to come up with terrible answers, which just might surface the best answers.

By now you are thinking – this is way too much to expect lawyers to sit through. We can inspire lawyers to think creatively and teach them to fail until we're blue in the face, and they are still not going to turn into designers who are capable of working through this drawn-out five-step human-centered touchy feely blah blah blah design process. Of course they aren't. Among the traits of successful lawyers is a sense of urgency (a score of 71 for lawyers versus 50 for the rest of humanity). These folks are impatient and hate to have their time wasted. Imagine the eyerolls if we asked busy, successful lawyers to join a group hug with us for a week, or even a whole day. Not. Going. To. Happen.

That's where our Design Jam comes in. We've taken what we hope are the key elements of the design thinking process and filtered them through our experience working with successful lawyers to create a Design Jam that is fun, engaging, and most of all, effective.

The Morgan Lewis eData Design Jam

We've assembled our teams and empowered their members. We've raised positive emotions and created inspiration, set up the right environment, convinced our legal design teams to meditate for a minute (maybe), and loosened everyone up by playing at fail camp.

It is time to jam!

The eData Design Jam is a guided team competition that uses an abbreviated version of the design thinking process to develop a prototype solution for a defined client problem. The team with the best design wins.

The eData Design Jam differs from traditional design in a few important ways. It's faster, for one, and it starts with a defined problem statement (in a typical design thinking exercise, the problem to be solved is studied and defined during the design process itself). I have learned – through painful experience – that it does not work to have teams that include lawyers free-associate about what the client's legal service delivery problem might be. Forty-five minutes later, you're almost out of time and everyone's still fighting about the definition of "legal service". Ugh.

So, we put some fencing around the problem by talking with the client and defining the problem statement ahead of time. For example, we might say, "Our clients frequently complain about the lack of transparency regarding our ongoing legal activities, fees, and costs. Those clients would like to have real-time, accurate, complete information about 'the work' we're doing for them. *How might we provide our clients with better access to this information?*"

We present that problem statement and give a short instructional talk on the design jam process, and then we hand out three boxes of random stuff and get everyone started.

Boxes? What boxes? Nobody said there'd be boxes.

Box one: Reimagine

This is the stage where we brainstorm potential solutions. The more creative, the better! First, we'll review both the problem statement and the rules of brainstorming. Then we'll dive into the first box, the Reimagine box. This box aims to create a sense of safety, fun, and play. It has a few actual toys in it to get the design team loosened up – pencils, crayons, markers, Play-Doh, things like that. We want to reduce cortisol production and get teams into a play state of mind.

We'll set a timer for ten minutes[26] and go for as many ideas as possible.

Box two: Redesign

In this step, our teams will evaluate their initial ideas. Which ones offer a high-impact, high-feasibility solution that should be explored further? Choose a few solutions and design rapid mock-ups of those solutions. In step two, we are making our ideas tangible by mapping out the user's journey with this solution. Identifying the pain points. Asking how this solution will solve them. Build a physical depiction of your potential solutions using the contents of the second box.

What's in the Redesign box? This is the planning and prototyping box. This box might have graph paper, rulers, tape, more markers, legos[27] and paper. Teams have a tendency to get stuck in the building phase. It is so foreign to their daily work that it's no wonder they stumble a bit. We have proctors at each table and people in each group who have more experience with design. They will lead by example, drawing things out and encouraging the team to illustrate their ideas. And there are legos. Nuff said.

Set the timer for another ten minutes and get building!

Box three: Re-engineer

It's time to pick one idea and refine it. Decide which solution represents your MVP (that's minimum viable product in design-speak). Give it a name and select a spokesperson who can pitch it to your client. Refine your prototype and document its features, value, and feasibility. Each team is preparing for two minutes in a "shark-tank" setting to make its case and set down a business plan for its chosen solution.

This is the stage where the team tests its solutions and seeks meaningful feedback from the client. The team uses the contents of the last box to distill the MVP's benefits. Our Re-engineer box has markers, posterboard, sketch pads and wireframe pads of an iPhone so the team can draw screen layouts if their solution is an app. The goal is to articulate the solution, how it is going to work and present the business case for your solution to the client at the table.

This can be a tough stage, because we often don't get it right the first time or the client may not like where we are going with the solution. It will feel rushed and our lawyers will hate to hear where we went wrong, but it is a critical part of the process and requires real listening and collaboration.

Set your timer for 20 minutes and get that pitch down.

The shark-tank

The end of the eData Design Jam process is the shark-tank. Each team gets to pitch its chosen concept to the group in a "shark-tank" setting, and the judges (the sharks can include the project sponsor, client legal and business leads, or practice group or firm leadership) proclaim a winner. Lawyers respond remarkably well to the shark-tank, and often self-select (with their team's blessing, of course) to be the spokesperson at the tank. But remember, no prizes! It's a biochemical thing: when you introduce money or stuff into the reward equation, you create the very stress – that cortisol spike – that you are trying so hard to reduce. Instead, we offer far more valuable rewards – recognition and opportunity (and hopefully some feel-good endorphins). Our winning team will often have the opportunity to implement their solution, whether it's working with our eData Rapid Development team to build their app or our eData AI Development team to build an algorithmic tool following the competition. They may present it as an MVP to the GC, or even a potential investor or developer. These are real stakes and real rewards.

That's the gist of the eData Design Jam – we have some fun, we rewire a few attorney brains to loosen up, and we design a thing. Oh, and if we're lucky, we make a client happy by hearing them, collaborating with them, showing them tangible value and delivering real, meaningful innovation. Maybe we even solve a problem.

References

1. Don Norman, *The Design of Everyday Things*, 1988.
2. www.dmi.org/page/DesignValue/The-Value-of-Design-.htm
3. www.mckinsey.com/business-functions/mckinsey-design/our-insights/the-business-value-of-design

4. Your fearless author would argue that there is no such thing as un-designed because all made things are designed, intentionally or otherwise. IMHO, a strong case can be made that most legal service delivery today is bad design. If that verdict is too harsh for your taste, let's agree that legal service delivery could be *vastly* improved and go from there.

5. The Legal Lean Sigma Institute is the leading provider of legal process improvement training and is unrivaled in this space. www.legalleansigma.com. See chapter 6 for more details.
6. Outside counsel guidelines are rife with examples of cost controls to address expenses that had always been an affront to common sense (or so I'm told by my in-house peers) but customary in legal: don't bill for travel time if you are just kicking it in first class and not actually working on our matter; don't send a busload of lawyers to a deposition; legal research, phone calls, faxes (please stop), and first years are your overhead, not ours. I could go on, but you get my (friend's) point.
7. Less stark reality, more nagging fear I'd venture. But, of course, that all depends on how prepared the particular firm is for the "big one".
8. I highly recommend Professor William Henderson's Report to the California Bar, the Legal Market Landscape report, which discusses these phenomena in detail. http://board.calbar.ca.gov/docs/agendaItem/Public/agendaitem1000022382.pdf
9. That will almost certainly and inevitably enable outside investment in and new law firm ownership structures.
10. I'd note that, besides making clients happy, legal design promises to increase profitability and create a competitive advantage and new revenue streams for law firms, all while weaning lawyers off the billable hour. That alone has not yet been deemed enough to drive adoption, but it does sound like a place we all want to visit, doesn't it?
11. This is far more radical than it sounds. Law firms strongly prefer to take a (Steve) Jobsian approach to clients: We know what's good for them. We will deliver to them what they need.
12. Ask my husband.
13. I'm a lawyer, so I'm talking about myself too, and #notalllawyers, sure. But if you're honest with yourself, and you are an attorney, you'll see a little of yourself in these traits.
14. www.lawyerbrain.com
15. See note 12.
16. Observing the lawyer score of 7, Dr Richard jokes, "Even a block of wood has eight percent sociability."
17. IDEO is the award-winning global design firm that I swear I'm not completely obsessed with. Or at least not in an unhealthy way. The smartest, coolest, nicest people on the planet work there and are doing great things in the world, including in legal. They also totally nailed brainstorming. www.ideou.com/pages/brainstorming
18. See https://seeincolors.com/a-simple-facilitation-technique-the-parking-lot/. I also learned about this meeting management technique from Catherine McDonough at www.legalleansigma.com, of course.
19. Now, seriously, chill the bleep out. There are no dinosaurs chasing you so relax. Get some Play-Doh or one of those fidget spinners or something.
20. Speaking of Zen, Dr Richard recommends meditation for lawyers. Don't stop reading! I felt the same way about meditation: I'm supposed to just turn off the dialogue that has been running through my head since 1982? No chance. But you

know what? Meditation works. Don't overthink it (zinga!) and I promise you can keep it short. Oh, and there's an app for that.

21. If you don't think it's possible to design for joy, I strongly encourage you to read *Joyful* by Ingrid Fetell Lee, which Dr Richard recommended to me. Best book I've read in years.
22. Maybe not dog treats, but cookies? Yes, cookies work like a charm.
23. Another great book recommendation is *Inside the Box, A Proven System of Creativity for Breakthrough Results* by Drew Boyd and Jacob Goldenberg.
24. By the way, this paralysis also has a biochemical explanation. In response to fear or shock, our nervous system, in addition to churning out stress hormones, generates autonomic (what we feel as instinctual) physical responses that facilitate our ability to fight or flee. When we feel trapped and are unable to fight or flee, physiological freeze or fear paralysis can occur. Animals do it all the time and as it turns out, so do we.
25. We use fail camp as an exercise during our Design Jams but Cat Moon runs an actual Failure Camp for lawyers and legal innovation professionals at Vanderbilt Law's Program on Law + Innovation. Check out www.solivanderbilt.org/ .
26. Our Design Jams fill the time we have. We've done Jams as short as 90 minutes and as long as three hours. We do not use our design jam process for big, lengthy projects that may fill days or weeks (we use full-blown design thinking methodology, agile, LPM and Six Sigma methods for those). We designed this design jam process specifically to be fast and effective, with tangible results delivered in short order.
27. Legos are the duct tape of design thinking. Brilliant little pieces of plastic we all know and love. No instructions necessary: build me a car? Done. A desk that floats in water? Done. A solution to the billable hour? Well… Sean Blair (no relation) teaches a great training course called Lego Serious Play. www.serious.global/about/ His book is fantastic too. www.serious.global/serious-work-how-to-facilitate-lego-serious-play/

Chapter 10:

How design thinking makes for good business development

By Mark Beese, president, Leadership for Lawyers llc

Nat Slavin is a partner in the Wicker Park Group, a consultancy focused on helping law firms strengthen and deepen their relationships with in-house counsel through client feedback and other client-facing programs. Nat has met with more than a thousand law firm clients – in-house counsel, chief legal officers, legal operations executives and business leaders – getting feedback on what drives the most successful relationships and greatest client loyalty. What do clients want from their outside counsel? Nat boils it down to three points:

> *"Beyond delivering quality legal advice, they want outside counsel to 1) demonstrate an understanding of their business and goals, 2) make their life easier, and 3) be enjoyable to work with. Doing those three things really drives loyalty, and keeps outside counsel top of mind."*

Recent surveys of in-house counsel have revealed that clients are looking to their outside counsel for innovative ways to be more efficient and effective through the re-design of traditional legal processes, the use of technology, leveraging ASPs, and other techniques. Sadly, outside counsel rarely deliver on these expectations, leaving corporate legal departments to drive innovation and legal process design, often at the expense of outside legal counsel.

How can design thinking improve client relationships and make for good business development? Let's look at the five stages of design thinking and see how they might benefit the attorney–client relationship. For this sake of this chapter, I will refer to lawyers and legal professionals who are engaged in design thinking as "legal designer" or "designer". The legal designer can be either an individual from a client or law firm, and can be in any role, including lawyer, executive, or staff.

Empathy

In this first stage, through observation and dialogue, legal designers gain a deeper understanding of their client's needs, wants, pain points and business context. This activity helps the legal designer gain a greater understanding of the client and her/his needs.

How might this look in real life? Let's say that a client is looking to reduce legal expenses by streamlining the legal process for a certain type of matter. While it might be tempting to simply give a discount rate, or replace a partner with a lower cost associate or contract attorney, a legal designer might see it as an opportunity to learn more about the client.

Our legal designer might start by interviewing everyone involved in these types of matters, on both the client and law firm side. What is your role in the matter? What works well when dealing with matters like this? What drives you crazy? What are the factors that slow down the process? What steps are not really necessary? Who must approve what? How long does each step take?

If the legal matter involves a behavior or situation that is observable (such as slip-and-falls at a grocery store), the legal designer might visit a few stores during a snowstorm and watch what a typical store might do to prevent injuries.

Sometimes a client's culture impacts a legal process. For example, by being overly cautious, requiring multiple levels of review, comment, and approval or by being unresponsive, letting emails, phone messages, and work product sit for weeks before being addressed, clients can significantly impact the efficiency and cost of a matter.

Likewise, a firm's culture can equally impact a legal process. Reward incentives, such as the billable hour system, can impact how long a matter takes to process. The propensity for lawyers and legal professionals to not leverage technology to reduce legal process time through automation can also impact the efficiency of a legal process. The legal designer might want to talk to executives on both the client and law firm side to identify potential cultural impacts on the process.

The designer might also want to seek an outside expert's view. This could be someone who is experienced in automating legal processes, or a legal operations executive from a non-competing company, or a management consultant with industry experience. They may be able to provide insight into the challenges facing the design team.

The goal of the legal designer is to see the problem with a fresh set of eyes, setting aside previous notions of why things work or not. She is looking for "red flag areas" that get people worked up. Strong emotions often guide behaviors that cause or illuminate problems.

Through interviews, observation, and involving outside experts, the legal designer can start to develop a model of what is happening now, and identify areas for improvement. Process maps and journey maps are great tools for this. By deeply understanding the current situation, the designer can begin to see where to focus her problem-solving efforts.

Imagine the legal designer meeting with her client, and discussing what she has discovered and the insights she has gained from her research. Anyone who has attended client panels has heard the chorus, "Please understand our business better". Is there a better way to understand a client, its business and the context of its legal issues?

Problem definition

The second stage of design thinking is clearly defining the problem you are trying to solve. The legal designer uses insights gained from the empathy stage to frame the problem not only in the legal context, but also in the context of solving a business or legal process problem, as the example above illustrates. Often the problems legal professionals need to help solve are not just legal in nature; rather they are complex issues that require creative thinking and innovative solutions.

The Hasso Plattner Institute of Design at Stanford (d.School) uses a concept called "Point of View (POV)". The POV is a guiding statement that focuses on specific users, insights, and needs that drives the design process. It is a simple, but crucial, statement that provides the focus and direction of the design process. For example, our legal designer in the example above recognizes that the client wants to save money and reduce the cycle time for these types of matters. However, her "Empathy Phase" activities revealed that the single most time- (and money-) wasting activity was repeated transmitted, review, comment, and revisions of documents. When things got busy (which was nearly all of the time), documents sometimes sat for days or weeks in an email folder, often frustrating one side or the other. Our legal designer identified several possible problems to address to meet her client's needs, but offered this as her Point of View:

> *"To create a document communication and review process that significantly reduces cycle time while improving the quality and accuracy of the contracts on a consistent basis, thus reducing the time to read emails, track changes, make changes, resulting in lower hours (and dollars) spent on these matters."*

Can you see how this provides focus to the problem and drives the next stages of the design process? Image what the client would say if their outside counsel came to them and said, "I'd like to focus our efforts in this area. I think it has the greatest potential to save time, money, and grief going forward. Do you want to work on this together?"

Sometimes the POV statement/problem definition is not obvious. Make sure that the POV statement is clearly derived from the pain points identified in the empathy stage. What one problem can we focus on solving that would have the most impact towards meeting the client's need? It may not be all things to all people.

Ideation

This is the brainstorming phase, best done in a group. Consider including representatives from the client's organization as well as outside experts in the process. The best brainstorming results in ideas that may be outside of lawyers' comfort zone. Have a discussion about preferences and risk tolerances and see if the team can stretch in its ability to think up truly innovative ideas. When clients and outside counsel come together to truly brainstorm, both are often pleasantly surprised at the creativity and willingness to push boundaries in the pursuit of an innovative solution.

After facilitating one such session in a Design Thinking Legal© workshop, a client said, "It is refreshing to see how well my outside lawyers have gone to not only understand our business and related legal challenges. I am very impressed with their insight and creativity to develop new ways to solve old problems. We made more progress in one afternoon than we have in the past five years."

One of the law firm lawyers in the same design group commented, "While I thought I knew their business, there was so much I didn't appreciate until we started the design process. I understand a lot more and I finally feel like part of their team."

Ideation in a team setting can not only result in better ideas, but can also build commitment to those in the design team. In an age where loyalty seems to be a rare commodity, using design thinking to develop innovative solutions can pay off with stronger ties between client and lawyer/law firm.

The ideation phase is not a time for any design team member to show off or try to "one-up" one another. Rather it is an opportunity for law firm lawyers and client representatives to practice collaboration and explore new ways to "do" legal work. Often, ideas are generated that might not apply to the problem at hand, but might be helpful in other ways. Look for ways to build off each other's ideas (think, "Yes, and..." rather than, "But, or...").

Using tools like "How might we?" questions can often spark engaging and productive brainstorm sessions. Using the earlier example, we could ask:

- How might we put the entire review process online and take it out of email?
- How might we do the entire process in 24 hours?
- How might we make a game out of it and assign points for responsiveness and quality?
- How might we automate the 80 percent of these documents that never change?
- How might we review, comment, approve and move along the process on an iPhone?

As the group considers the results of the brainstorm and begins to select ideas for prototyping, look for opportunities for both collaboration and innovation. Don't settle on the easiest path. Challenge the team to find a novel solution that can be both beautiful in its design and effective in its application. Work on ways to build commitment and enthusiasm for the ideas moving forward.

Can you think of a better way to deepen a relationship with a client and outside counsel? The team is jointly working towards solving an important client problem. Both parties are collaborating and playing off each other's ideas. Everyone is envisioning how ideas might play out in real life, and anticipating that the design team will be involved in implementing the solution.

Prototyping

In this phase, the design team mocks up a physical manifestation or process for examination and evaluation. It is an iterative process of trial and error, with each progressive iteration showing the design team how to improve the design based on feedback from the user(s). The iterative process can be maddening, but it not only refines the solution, it builds strong bonds between the client and outside counsel.

Often, a legal design solution involves a new process. Sometimes this involves technology, but not always. The process prototype can be illustrated in a process map, Gantt chart, journey map, or some other representation. The legal designer can then "test" the prototypes by walking various stakeholders through the process to get their feedback.

This is a valuable experience for the designer, as it will give her insight into the preferences and priorities of various people in the client organization. Imagine taking a prototype idea to not only the legal department, but also the client's finance, marketing, and operational units for feedback and insight.

One of my favorite feedback tools is the Feedback Capture Grid (shown below). When seeking feedback, ask stakeholders:

- What do you like about this solution? (+)
- What would you change to this solution? (Δ)
- What questions do you have? What confuses you? (?)
- What interests or excites you the most about this solution? (⚡)

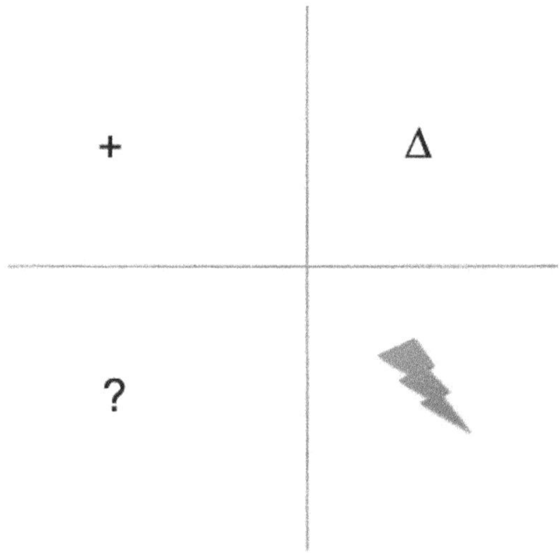

Beware of idea-killing dragons in this phase. Often you are testing new, out-of-the-box ideas with stakeholders who are not part of the design team. They may be skeptical and risk adverse. They may not have drunk the "design thinking cool-aid" yet. Don't be discouraged by these dragons. Rather, use their insights to both improve your solution and prepare your launch strategy. Their skepticism will give you clues on how to craft your message and build alliances when you launch your innovative idea.

Honesty, authenticity, and conflict over ideas (not personalities) is encouraged at all phases, but this one especially. These values improve the result and build trust among team members, especially between clients and their outside counsel. Don't hide under a rock, nor should you shy from conflict that might lead to a better outcome.

As you seek feedback and revise your innovation, use the experience to share feedback with the design team and collaborate on the next iteration. Remember that the goal is not only to solve the problem, but also to build commitment among the team to make it a reality. The feedback you receive and the diverse relationships you build as a designer will open doors for new opportunities with the client long after the design project is implemented.

Beta testing

Early in the design thinking process we prototype for empathy – i.e. we share prototype ideas to get feedback on the idea so we can make iterative improvements. Later in the process we prototype for feasibility. This is the testing phase.

Taking an idea from a prototype to a testing environment requires a different set of skills. Legal designers need to practice strong project management skills and a willingness to be flexible in trying new approaches. If possible, find metrics that can indicate whether progress is being made over the existing system. For example, cycle time between benchmarks, billable time dedicated to specific tasks, wait or down time between key tasks, etc.

Lawyers are taught in law school not to release a work product unless it is flawless. Design thinking doesn't work that way. It is an iterative process that tests a solution, makes revisions, and tests again until feasibility is confirmed. This may be challenging for some members of the design team, and may require some discipline and vulnerability to introduce design thinking mindsets to the organization.

Designers from law firms (whether lawyers or business professionals) have an opportunity to display their project management and collaboration skills, creativity, and political savvy in this phase, building confidence and loyalty from clients.

Client relationships result from design thinking

Clients and outside counsel can expect that innovation through the design thinking process will be hard work, resulting in both innovative solutions and increased collaboration. Clients will gain a greater appreciation for how their outside counsel can help them solve complex problems (legal and business). After investing time into the design process, clients will develop a deeper loyalty to their outside counsel, characterized by increased trust and communication about difficult topics.

Law firm lawyers and business professionals will gain a better understanding of their client's business, industry, context, challenges, and service preferences. With this increased understanding, lawyers will be better able to offer services and solutions that meet the specific needs and preferences of their clients (opposed to "cross-selling").

Together, both parties will benefit from more honest and effective communication, as they've been dealing with frank feedback from all quarters during an innovation project. Finally, as the client–law firm design team concept progresses, both parties benefit from developing new ways to efficiently and profitably deliver legal services.

So, what do you think? Nat Slavin said that clients want outside counsel to 1) demonstrate an understanding of their business and goals, 2) make their life easier, and 3) be enjoyable to work with. Can design thinking help you, your firm, or legal department meet these expectations? I think the design thinking is a "killer app" for business development and client service success.

Chapter 11: Designing your legal career

By R. Amani Smathers, senior legal solutions architect at Davis Wright Tremaine, and Amy Monaghan, practice innovations manager at Perkins Coie

Introduction

> *"Tell me, what will you do with that one precious and wild* legal brain *of yours?"*[1]

Bernadette Bulacan recently posed the above question (paraphrasing poet Mary Oliver) to the attendees of the Law Jobs for Humans 2.0 conference.[2] If it feels like a daunting question, you're in the right place. In this chapter, we share how to flip design thinking around to focus on your own values and needs, and in the process, intentionally design a fulfilling career for yourself.

With a continuous improvement mindset, everyone has room for growth. Whether you are new to your career or experienced, you may feel as though you still haven't found what it is that you want to do "when you grow up," or you may feel stuck. If you are successfully building a legal career you love, there may still be areas of your work, health, or personal life where you would like to shift focus to achieve an improved whole. Perhaps you have successfully designed your career and you are now in a position where you get to build a team. We have also included tips for using design thinking processes to iterate on team structure.

Margaret Hagan, director of the Legal Design Lab at Stanford, describes design thinking as a new pair of glasses. She says design thinking "offers you mindsets that will help you see the challenge area with greater insight, and get to promising ideas and prototypes with more efficiency and chance of success".[3] Just like you can learn to "think like a lawyer," you can learn to "think like a designer".[4] The design thinking mindset and process can help us tackle pain points for our clients – and also help us identify career paths that put us in the position to improve others' experiences with the legal system and build rewarding careers for ourselves.

In pursuit of a fulfilling career and a life well lived

Designers like tackling big challenges, and there are few more universal questions than how to achieve a life well lived. In their book *Designing Your Life: How to Build a Well-Lived, Joyful Life*, authors Bill Burnett and Dave Evans provide practical methods for applying design thinking to craft a "personally meaningful and authentic, as well as commercially viable" career.[5] They have honed their exercises and tips through years of teaching courses and workshops on the topic at the Stanford d.school (more formally, the Hasso Plattner Institute of Design).

The Pew Research Center reports that 95 percent of American teens say having a career they enjoy will be extremely or very important to them as an adult.[6] Only half that number expect getting married or having children will be important to them.[7] But how do we achieve a satisfying career? As one user-experience designer pointed out, "Although people often think about choosing the right school to attend or job to seek, you should *really think about the kind of life experience you're seeking*".[8]

Ultimately, the specifics of a fulfilling career will be different for everyone, but research has identified three factors that significantly motivate us and lead to personal satisfaction:

- Autonomy: The desire to be self-directed; to have control over our actions and situation.
- Mastery: The desire to develop (and continue developing) important skills.
- Purpose: The desire to do something that has meaning to ourselves and others.[9]

Certainly, a career in law can tick these boxes. If or when it does not tick them for you, however, it may be time for a career pivot.[10] A common misconception is that "there's only one right solution or optimal version of your life, and that if you choose wrong, you've blown it".[11] Burnett and Evans dispute that idea and encourage their life design students and readers to reframe goals as identifying *an* optimal version of their lives.[12] Reassuringly, there is not a single right answer for you; there are many potential ways to build a meaningful life and career for yourself.

Our experience – opportunity in ambiguity

What led us to contribute this chapter to a book on design thinking for legal professionals? Amy and Amani are both six years into careers in legal technology, knowledge management, and the broader area of law firm innovation. We have walked what is, as Professor William Henderson has described it, less of a defined career path and "more like following some matted grass".[13] We, like designers, have found opportunity in ambiguity.

We entered law school following the Great Recession and amid uncertainty about the value of a law school degree. Students who had graduated earlier the same year were struggling to find legal jobs, a fact that numerous scholars were showing to be not only the result of macroeconomic forces affecting the nationwide economy but also – more ominously for law grads, perhaps – representative of fundamental changes in the market for legal services.[14]

It was in the context of the poor legal market of the early 2010s that Professors Renee Knake and Daniel Martin Katz started the ReInvent Law Laboratory at Michigan State University (MSU) College of Law, focused on bringing together law, technology, design thinking, and new service delivery models.[15] Professor Knake often explains that one of her key motivations for co-founding ReInvent Law was to help her students find "rewarding and meaningful" careers in law.[16] Knake and Katz taught their ReInvent Law students (including Amani) about the holistic legal industry. They infused entrepreneurship into their courses to improve students' understanding of the legal profession and to give students new options for defining their future roles in it. ReInvent Law students learned that there was a lot of opportunity in the legal space – especially if they were willing to be entrepreneurial with their career paths. While Amani was first exposed to design thinking as a discipline in law school, Amy researched and learned design thinking methods out of personal and professional interest. Both have applied design thinking processes and mindsets to projects at their firms.

Amani and Amy are not professional development practitioners nor life coaches. We have applied the design thinking mindset in our own work, and we recognize the value of design thinking practices for helping individuals intentionally create meaningful and rewarding lives. We aim to share those practices in this chapter.

We also are not trying to discourage anyone from being a lawyer, as we know many amazing attorneys who have found fulfillment practicing law. We hope these tools and mindsets, wherever they may lead you, will help you build a fulfilling career for yourself. If you are currently seeking a change, perhaps you would find more fulfillment in a different area of law or in a different environment, such as a larger or smaller law firm or company. Or, maybe it is time to think further outside the JD-required box. It depends on what is likely to make you thrive – and applying design thinking to "life design" can help you open up more options and find opportunity in ambiguity.

The related fields of design, design thinking, legal design, and life design

Design thinking is a mindset and a set of practices for product and service creation and creative problem solving, keenly focused on user experience. Visual design, product design, architectural design, and system design are professions unto themselves. Design *thinking* allows us to use elements of design in our own professions and broader contexts.[17] Design firm IDEO has used design thinking methods to tackle challenges from creating the first manufacturable mouse for Apple to combating food waste to designing an accessible voting experience for voters in Los Angeles County.[18] The firm uses design thinking (also called human-centered design) practices to tackle "big questions" including "How can we use AI to make things better for humans?" and "How can government be more citizen-focused?"[19]

Margaret Hagan founded the Legal Design Lab at Stanford to build new solutions for legal services, particularly for access to justice.[20] She explains that design thinking can be used by "any person in the legal sector who wants to serve their clients better, who wants to improve their own work life and organization, and who wants to see better kinds of work product, service delivery, and ecosystems in law".[21] Hagan's web book *Law by Design* covers the design "mindsets, process, and mechanics" that offer structured ways to identify key challenges people face with participating effectively in the current legal system. Once those challenges are identified, the same design processes can be used to create innovative solutions.

Unlike consumer design, which is focused on persuading users to consume a product or services, Hagan says that legal design is aimed at helping users navigate the complex, often obtuse legal systems. Legal design is "aimed at the brain" and how to increase a person's capacity to "make smart decisions for their long-term interests."

Similarly, Burnett and Evans apply design thinking to life design, helping people identify a path toward creating a life and career through which they can continuously build meaning and fulfillment. Their recommended methods are in line with the general design thinking process.

The design thinking process is typically broken out into five to seven modes. IDEO calls these "modes" rather than "phases" or "steps" to emphasize that they are not necessarily a linear, consecutive process.

Designers can loop back and forth between the modes as needed. At a high level, the modes include:[22]

1. **Empathize** (Discovery): Conduct research and develop a deep understanding of your users;
2. **Define**: Synthesize your research and define the key challenge that you seek to address, and some goal posts for what success could look like;
3. **Ideate**: Generate a range of creative ideas – including the wild and crazy ones;
4. **Prototype**: Build real, tactile representation of a few ideas;
5. **Test**: Gather user feedback on prototypes;
6. **Implement:** Put the solution into effect. (Some diagrams of the design thinking process actually leave this off – but it's the ultimate goal! We learn and ideate and prototype and test so that we can implement a solution that thrills our users!); and
7. **Iterate** (Evolution): Scale, pivot, or tweak the design based on how users interact with the solution, better ideas, or new needs. A good solution goes stale – we have to keep it fresh by iteratively improving.

Using the work of Burnett, Evans, and Hagan as a backdrop, we devote the following section to laying out how you can apply design thinking to your career planning toolkit. Grab some extra paper, pens, and maybe some sticky notes – it's time to try putting the life design process into action!

Applying the design process – your legal career design toolkit

(Self) discovery and empathy – *interview and observe yourself for greater understanding of what a successful life means to you.*

The first mode in the design thinking process is discovery, also referred to as the empathy mode. In solution design, this involves conducting user interviews (with lots of "why" questions) and observing users so that you can get a deep understanding of their habits, values, and needs. Understanding users at this deep level helps designers create products and services that meet the most fundamental needs, perhaps even beyond those that the users clearly express.

This is relevant to life design as well as solution design because, as individuals, we aren't always the best designers for ourselves when we are not being intentional. Burnett and Evans explain that their discovery method “surfaces stuff that people haven’t worked through yet”, and asks questions that “no one really asked them yet”, including themselves.[23]

To help clarify your work and life values, here are some sample questions to ask yourself about what matters to you. Don’t just think about your answers; write them down for reference later.

- What is your “definition of success” for a [legal] career?
- Is it important to you to practice law, and why?
- What is it about practicing law that inspires you, and why?
- Who are three people that you would like to work with or for, and why?
- How important is compensation to you, and why?
- How important is external recognition to you, in what form is it most important, and why?
- What roles do family, culture, and other social aspects play in how you view your work and your life?

If you already know what you are passionate about, great – but if you don’t feel particularly passionate about a professional area, let yourself off the hook. Burnett and Evans say that, in their experience, about 80 percent of people of all ages do not know what they’re passionate about. It takes time to develop a passion, and passion is the *result* of a good life design and experience, not the *cause*.[24] Research also suggests that pursuing passions outside of our career can lead to greater holistic benefits.[25]

Next, observe your actions. The Stanford d.school’s process guide on design thinking points out that “[s]ome of the most powerful realizations come from noticing a disconnect between what someone says and what he does”.[26] The same is true when applying design thinking to oneself as the “user”. So, to observe yourself in the context of both your work and your personal life, Burnett and Evans suggest keeping a “Good Time Journal” (GTJ) for three weeks.

In the GTJ, create a log of your activities each day. For each activity, note a 1 to 10 rating of your engagement level (1 meaning low/bored; 10 meaning high/achieving “flow”) and your energy level (1 meaning negative energy/draining; 10 meaning very positive/energizing). At the end of each week, review your entries to categorize the activities that energized you, the ones that drained you, and the ones during which you felt intensely engaged and "in the zone" (designers call this a state of "flow").[27]

If the prospect of recording your activities for three weeks is a nonstarter for you, try to find a way to at least catalog those things that left you energized and those that didn't. One easy way to do this is to look at your calendar at the end of each day and note which tasks or meetings fall into which category. Do this for a timeframe that works for you; you can also expand the timeframe further and consider moments of flow over past years.[28] The point is to gather data that will help you observe which activities to double down on and which to avoid as you pursue a career that will be enjoyable and fulfilling.

Burnett and Evans provide an example of a man named Michael, who had followed his mother's plan for him to become a civil engineer and was happy in his career for a while, until he wasn't. His father-in-law suggested a move into finance as another career that would make use of his math skills, so Michael started to consider quitting his job to attend business school. After working on his GTJ, however, "Michael discovered that he actually enjoyed civil engineering. It was the people stuff, the proposal writing, and the fee negotiations that he hated." So instead of business school (which may have led him into a career focused on exactly the activities that drained him), he entered a PhD program and became a high-level engineer, allowing him to focus on solving complex engineering problems, which he loves. He didn't have to make a big career pivot, but he did have to intentionally observe his energy and engagement in everyday activities to empathize with himself. Only then could he design his career in a way that would align his work with what fulfilled him.[29]

When making decisions about what type of job to pursue after law school, Amani considered the courses and activities that had given her "flow". Typically an A-student, a couple of Bs in math and science courses in high school scared her away from pursuing a STEM major in college. And yet, some of her most memorable moments of flow occurred when working on statistics projects to find meaning in data and when problem solving to create simple applications in a computer science elective. In law school, she learned how to think like a lawyer, but she found greater engagement learning about the business of law. She was drained by legal research and writing. So, when considering whether to pursue a traditional legal career after law school, she decided that the surface-level credibility she might gain by racking up years of practice wasn't worth heading away from her True North. Instead, she headed straight toward it by accepting a nontraditional role in the Legal Technology Innovations Office of an Am Law 100 firm.

Another example in the legal space is Amy's boss, Gwyn McAlpine. Gwyn, director of knowledge management services at Perkins Coie, was a business associate focusing on M&A and securities compliance. When the time came for Gwyn to decide if she was going to pursue a partner track, she decided that was not necessarily in line with her career values. Instead, she pivoted to a knowledge management role. At first, she split her time 50/50 – half practicing and half providing knowledge management services for the group. As a one-woman KM department, this became unsustainable, and she ultimately chose to pursue KM full-time. Gwyn has been able to build an entire department, and through heading that rapidly growing team, she has become an industry leader because she decided to design an alternative path.

Using design thinking may not mean you need to find an alternative to practicing law; rather, it may help highlight different areas of law or clients that you want to focus on. The stories are meant to illustrate that by paying attention and taking inventory of what engages you in your current or past roles, you can home in on those activities that bring you satisfaction and energize you. Please remember to have empathy for yourself during this exercise. It can be easy to dwell on past decisions or relitigate old issues. Remember these wise words: "Sometimes you're ahead, sometimes you're behind. The race is long and, in the end, it's only with yourself."[31]

Synthesis – build your compass

Burnett and Evans call the GTJ a "wayfinding" activity, in that it can help you figure out where you are going when you don't know your destination.[32] Typically, the second mode of the design thinking process is described as the define phase, in which you synthesize all the information you gathered about your users' values and needs, and then distill it into an explicit expression of the problem you want to address.[33] In life design, the definition of success is not meant to be a specific statement such as, "I want to be general counsel at ABC Company by age 40," but instead a description of your values and some guardrails that will help you determine whether you are on or off track toward a career that you will find fulfilling.

Burnett and Evans recommend defining your "True North" by writing out your lifeview, your workview, and insights about where they complement each other or clash. Ultimately, they say, bringing your lifeview and workview into harmony will "increase your own clarity and ability to live a consciously coherent, meaningful life."[34] Insights from your GTJ also contribute to your definition of life success by serving as a compass to tell you when you are heading in your right direction.

When Amy was narrowing in on what she wanted to pursue after law school, she did a similar exercise by listing all the things she valued professionally and personally. Among the overlapping values were creativity and autonomy. Around the same time, she was learning how to build systems to help increase efficiency and accuracy in legal work and found that she really enjoyed this work as it combined her analytical abilities with her creativity. Rather than continuing to focus on practicing roles, she decided to align her job search with her interests in data and automation, which led her to a knowledge management role. This set Amy on a path to build a career where her creativity is valued and encouraged, which has led to greater autonomy in her roles.

As a result of your GTJ and definition of success, you may have an idea that one way to get to your True North is not necessarily by changing your career, but instead by redesigning your legal practice. There are many reasons why you may be looking to change your practice. You may want to create new business models that are attractive to clients and profitable for you. You may want to try to "productize" your expertise to offer your work to a greater volume of clients.[35] You can certainly use design thinking for that, and the processes described below can be a guide.

Similarly, you may love your work but find that the reason you are not fulfilled is because you do not have the right resources to feel fully supported, leading you to overwork and potentially burn out. If this is the situation, you may want to focus your design efforts on building a team to scale your work, or on identifying areas for efficiency gains. In this context, define your compass according to the direction you want to build your resources toward.

Ideate – create choices

Once you have interviewed and observed yourself and identified your definition of a meaningful and fulfilling life, the next step is to ideate many possible ways of getting there. As Burnett and Evans remind us, there is no single right answer for any of us; there are many careers we could pursue to live a meaningful life. So, in this stage, the goal is to *create choices*.

Tips for ideating include:

- "Make a bad idea": free yourself from the pressure to create good ideas; remove the risk from the activity by creating a couple of throwaways;[36]
- Focus on quantity over quality for early ideation;

- Don't fall in love with your first idea – it's rarely the best;[37]
- Resist judging yourself[38] and ideate like nobody's watching;
- Ask yourself, "How might I…?" followed by challenges you foresee in heading toward your True North or dream goals. For example, "How might I develop and grow a career that lets me live or travel abroad the majority of my time?"
- At the same time, *don't filter out* ideas based on concerns of "How could I possibly…?" Pause feasibility questions at this stage.[39] Write down the crazy idea. Sometimes great solutions develop later on from taking an "out there" idea and scaling it back just enough to make it actionable; and
- Imagine an amazing, unbelievable headline written about a fictional achievement of yours. What does the article say?

From your list of ideas, circle words or select concepts that stick out to you as the most interesting. Invent three possible careers from them. Sketch images that represent these careers. Note that these ideas don't need to be practical, so keep your internal critic at bay – you're still ideating! You are *not problem solving* right now, you are ideating. What can you imagine?

Once you have given yourself space to be creative and you have created a number of ideas ("diverged"), then it is time to make choices ("converge") focused on a few top contenders. Burnett and Evans recommend this model for developing three alternative career paths:

- Life One: Expand on your current favorite idea or your current career. This is the main idea you already have.
- Life Two: Imagine what you would do if Life One wasn't an option. What would keep you pointed toward your True North and allow you to make a living?
- Life Three: Imagine what you would do if money and image didn't matter. Beyond those two things, what matters most to you? What career path might let you live out those work and life values?

Burnett and Evans then recommend mapping out these three lives in phased drawings of alternative versions of your next five years, which they call Odyssey Planning.

Another way to diverge is to categorize your many ideas into three overlapping categories, Venn diagram-style:

- What I do well;
- What people will me pay for; and
- What I want to do.[40]

Your current sweet spot is at the center of that Venn diagram – although, if there is an idea that really speaks to you in one of the nonoverlapping sections, you don't have to rule it out. Make that your Life Three option. It may take more time to achieve, but short-term prototypes will help you determine whether additional time investments will likely lead to greater life fulfillment.

You can also use the above exercises to ideate team building and resource gathering for redesigning your practice. Instead of three alternative careers, identify three alternative teams (including team size, specialties, levels of skill, etc.) or three alternative tracks of resources you can focus on building to meet your practice needs.

Prototype and test – gain experiences and evaluate

The next phase of designing your life involves prototyping your ideas in such a way that you can test them. Prototypes allow an actual experience of an idea. Significant literature exists about ideas for prototyping products and services.[41] Likewise, many software tools are available to help designers create levels of prototypes, from low-fidelity wireframe mockups to high-fidelity models that look and feel like the real thing. Burnett and Evans suggest a couple of ideas for prototyping your life design on a similar scale.

On the low-fidelity end, they recommend simply imagining yourself on one of those career paths. When you brush your teeth, imagine you are on that path. When you drive to work, imagine you are driving to that job. How do you feel? What are you excited or worried about? Over the next few days, imagine yourself on another career path that you want to try out. Do you feel differently? Which one feels more directionally on point for your True North?

When you have narrowed your ideas to one that you want to invest more time and energy into prototyping, Burnett and Evans recommend finding people with jobs in that space and engaging in informational interviews. Interviews, in this context, are really just conversations. Find out from these conversations what it's like to have a particular job, but don't talk about your own career search—at least not right away. Burnett and Evans note that once you identify yourself as a potential job candidate, your conversation partner will shift into critique mode to assess you. Instead, the goal is for you to learn what it would be like to have that person's role, and use that individual's experiences as a prototype that you can mentally test against your own True North. By researching your potential career pivot in this manner, you also have the opportunity to grow your professional network in a way that will be critical once you get to the implement mode.

In the context of designing a team, prototyping can include experimenting with alternative staffing models until you've landed on the right design for your needs. Over the last two years, we (Amy and her team at Perkins Coie) have used this approach while staffing up our Practice Innovations team. We participated in an MSU College of Law class that involved working with 12 students on legal innovation projects. That, in turn, led to us creating two internship opportunities to continue some of the work that began during the semester-long class. The internships led to creation of a year-long Practice Innovations Fellowship, which we opened to recent law graduates, and also resulted in our participation as an employer in a seven-month internship program with the Institute for the Future of the Law Profession ("IFLP").[42] Each of these lower-risk experimentations helped us learn about our needs and capabilities and allowed us to gain a clearer picture of our longer-term staffing plans in light of the opportunities we are pursuing.

Another lower-risk team-prototype tactic you may want to consider is building unofficial cross-functional teams within your organization. This does not require formal structural changes and can allow you to prove out concepts and ideas about team structure that will ultimately help you design your team. Start small by pulling in people from various functions on a project or mini-project basis. Keep iterating on the team's makeup and duties and "fail forward," meaning that you will use every "failure" as an opportunity to learn and grow.[43] Speaking of growth, when looking for team members, seek out people with a growth mindset, as that perspective is a critical characteristic of a high-performing team.[44]

Implement – put your career design into action

Once you've landed on the life design you want to pursue, it's time to implement it. If your design involves changing jobs, you'll likely need to navigate the "hidden job market," which actually accounts for most available jobs.[45] This means you will need to rely on, and most likely grow, your network, especially if your design involves transitioning to a new area of focus. Networking in this context does not necessarily mean attending an awkward networking reception. There are other (better!) ways to network through specialized avenues such as Twitter,[46]

LinkedIn, professional association conferences and local events, and targeted conversations with people in your new focus area.

Your design might involve an internal shift within your current organization. If you are interested in an area where your firm or legal department has a need (or you see a need that hasn't yet been identified), look for people to discuss these opportunities with, and plant seeds for pursuing that path. Some examples could include transitioning to a nonpracticing role within a knowledge management or library department or pursuing legal project management or practice management roles. Similarly, there is a growing demand for legal operations professionals within corporate legal departments.[47]

Making transitions can be difficult, and it always comes with an uncertainty cost (although hopefully your prototyping will contribute to a smooth transition). Remember to have empathy with yourself and those who are on this journey with you. Especially with newer roles in the legal field, there may not be a well-paved path for you to follow. Don't give in to "impostor syndrome".[48] When you're walking a "matted grass" path, so few are going before you that there are aren't even many to live up to; you are creating your career and your path. It may be helpful to remember a few lines from the most prolific life-advice expert, Dr. Seuss: "Today you are you, that is truer than true. There is no one alive who is you-er than you. Shout loud, I am lucky to be what I am. Thank goodness I'm not just a clam or a ham, or a dusty old jar of sour gooseberry jam. I am what I am, what a great thing to be. If I say so myself, happy [everyday] to me!"[49]

Iterate – build forward

Once you've implemented your well-designed life, you're not done. "Life is a joyous and never-ending design project of building your life forward."[50] You will be constantly iterating to account for new circumstances, including life and career shifts. You will also be checking in with yourself consistently and asking where you can find further opportunities for design. Especially in new fields or "alternative" careers, you may continue to encounter ambiguity in your role, even after you land it. Reframe that ambiguity in your mind as opportunity. Intrapreneurship can lead to exciting opportunities and a chance to create truly impactful innovation.[51] Your entire department may continue iterating and pivoting as it experiments, fails, and reinvents itself. For example, when interviewing for her first law firm role as a Legal Solutions Architect at Seyfarth Shaw, Amani was explicitly told that she should not expect the department she hired into to be the same in six to 12 months. It was constantly evolving (and the interviewers were screening for candidates who could tolerate, or even thrive on, ambiguity).

Flourishing in an uncertain and ever-changing role requires grit and resilience.[52] When hiring new team members, both Amani and Amy screen for grit and resilience in the people they interview. For survival beyond even a few years, adaptiveness and evolution are key. Make sure that you are consistently "building your way forward."[53] As with solution design, you will need to check in with your "end user" (yourself) and iterate as necessary.

References

1. *See* https://twitter.com/InHouse_Bern/status/1195505617647153157; https://twitter.com/QuantumJurist/status/1195584597431668736 (emphasis added).
2. Law Jobs for Humans is an event aimed at bringing together and supporting legal innovators "forging new and unique careers at the frontier of the legal sector." For more on Law Jobs for Humans, see https://abovethelaw.com/legal-innovation-center/2019/09/09/announcing-law-jobs-for-humans-2-0/.
3. Margaret Hagan, *Law by Design*, http://www.lawbydesign.co/en/legal-design/ (last visited 26 November 2019).
4. *Id.*
5. Bill Burnett and Dave Evans, *Designing Your Life: How to Build a Well-Lived, Joyful Life* (2016).
6. Juliana Menasce Horowitz and Nikki Graf, *Most US Teens See Anxiety and Depression as a Major Problem Among Their Peers: For boys and girls, day-to-day experiences and future aspirations vary in key ways*, Pew Research Center (20 February 2019), available at www.pewsocialtrends.org/2019/02/20/most-u-s-teens-see-anxiety-and-depression-as-a-major-problem-among-their-peers/. Despite the title, this article reports on a general survey of teens' values and concerns.
7. *Id.* In contrast to the nearly ubiquitous aspiration of an enjoyable career, far fewer teens reported that they expect getting married (only 47 percent) and having children (only 39 percent) to be important priorities for themselves when they grow up.
8. D. Ben Woods, *Book Review: Designing Your Life* (26 August 2019), www.uxmatters.com/mt/archives/2019/08/book-review-designing-your-life.php (emphasis added).
9. *See* Daniel Pink, *Drive: The Surprising Truth About What Motivates Us* (2009). For a ten-minute overview by the author, see: www.youtube.com/watch?v=u6XAPnuFjJc. Similarly, other studies have shown that the work traits that lead to career satisfaction are control, creativity, and impact. *See* Cal Newport, *So Good They Can't Ignore You: Why Skills Trump Passion in the Quest for Work You Love* (2012).
10. For more guidance on career pivots, see Jenny Blake, *Pivot: The Only Move That Matters Is Your Next One* (2016).

11. Steven Kurutz, "Want to Find Fulfillment at Last? Think Like a Designer", *New York Times* (17 September 2016), www.nytimes.com/2016/09/18/fashion/design-thinking-stanford-silicon-valley.html?_r=0.
12. Reframing a challenge from a different perspective can unlock many new possible solutions, and is a common technique in design thinking. Tina Seelig gives the simple example of two questions: "What is the sum of 5 plus 5?" and "What two numbers add up to 10?" As Seelig points out, "The first question has only one right answer, and the second question has an infinite number of solutions, including negative numbers and fractions. ... [B]y changing the frame, you dramatically change the range of possible solutions." Tina Seelig, *How Reframing A Problem Unlocks Innovation*, Fast Company (19 April 2013), available at www.fastcompany.com/1672354/how-reframing-a-problem-unlocks-innovation.
13. https://twitter.com/InHouse_Bern/status/1195411262022340616.
14. William Henderson and Rachel Zahorsky, "Law Job Stagnation May Have Started Before the Recession – And It May Be a Sign of Lasting Change" (1 July 2011) *ABA Law Journal*, available at www.abajournal.com/magazine/article/paradigm_shift; *see also* www.nytimes.com/2015/04/27/business/dealbook/burdened-with-debt-law-school-graduates-struggle-in-job-market.html; *see also* Deborah Jones Merritt, *What Happened to the Class of 2010? Empirical Evidence of Structural Change in the Legal Profession, Michigan State Law Review* 1043 (30 January 2016). Available at SSRN: https://ssrn.com/abstract=2577272 or http://dx.doi.org/10.2139/ssrn.2577272.
15. Professor Knake is now a professor of law and the Joanne and Larry Doherty Chair in Legal Ethics at the University of Houston Law Center. Professor Katz is now a professor of law and director of the Law Lab at Chicago Kent. Katz and Knake's early ReInvent Law program at MSU College of Law has evolved as the Legal RnD Lab and Center for Law, Technology & Innovation, www.law.msu.edu/lawtech.
16. *See* www.abajournal.com/legalrebels/article/2013_legal_rebel_profile_renee_knake/ and https://joseflegal.com/blog/interview-with-renee-knake-founder-of-one-of-the-first-law-labs/.
17. Hagan, *supra* note 3.
18. *See* www.ideo.com/about.
19. *See* www.ideo.com/questions.
20. *See* https://law.stanford.edu/organizations/pages/legal-design-lab/.
21. Hagan, *supra* note 3.
22. *See* Sarah Gibbons, *Design Thinking 101*, Nielsen Norman Group (31 July 2016), available at www.nngroup.com/articles/design-thinking/; Hagan, *supra* note 3, at www.lawbydesign.co/en/design-process/#1.
23. Steven Kurutz, "Want to Find Fulfillment at Last? Think Like a Designer", *New York Times* (17 September 2016) www.nytimes.com/2016/09/18/fashion/design-thinking-stanford-silicon-valley.html.
24. Burnett and Evans, *supra* note 5, at xxviii. *See also* Cal Newport, *So Good They Can't Ignore You: Why Skills Trump Passion in the Quest for Work You Love* (2012).

25. Jon M. Jachimowicz, Joyce He, and Julián Arango, "The Unexpected Benefits of Pursuing a Passion Outside of Work", *Harvard Business Review* (19 November 2019), available at https://hbr.org/2019/11/the-unexpected-benefits-of-pursuing-a-passion-outside-of-work?_lrsc=950c2746-f078-4539-a4f1-3263ac6a8826.
26. *See* Hasso Plattner Institute of Design at Stanford, *An Introduction to Design Thinking: Process Guide* (2010), https://dschool-old.stanford.edu/sandbox/groups/designresources/wiki/36873/attachments/74b3d/ModeGuideBOOTCAMP2010L.pdf.
27. Burnett and Evans, *supra* note 5, at 44. The authors also suggest further homing in on "the good stuff" by getting even more specific about what's working using the AEIOU method: identify details about the Activities, Environments, Interactions, Objects, and Users (other people and their roles) that were a part of the positive experiences. *See* Burnett and Evans, *supra* note 5, at 55.
28. If you go this route, though, beware of nostalgia. Be honest with yourself when reviewing "mountaintop moments" of the past. Burnett and Evans, *supra* note 5, at 58.
29. Burnett and Evans, *supra* note 5, at 48.
30. Journalist Mary Schmich's words of wisdom were recorded and gained popularity in a spoken word song released in 1999 by Baz Luhrmann, "Everybody's Free (To Wear Sunscreen)". You can read her original essay here: Mary Schmich, *Advice, like youth, probably just wasted on the young*, Chicago Tribune (1 June 1997), available at: www.chicagotribune.com/columns/chi-schmich-sunscreen-column-column.html.
31. Burnett and Evans, *supra* note 5, at 41.
32. *See supra* note 25.
33. Burnett and Evans, *supra* note 5, at 36.
34. If this is of interest to you, see the following article Amy and Jason Dirkx wrote for ILTA on this topic: Jason Dirkx and Amy Monaghan, *Lawyering in your sleep: An Approach to Legal Product Development*, Peer to Peer: ILTA's Quarterly Magazine (Spring 2019), available at http://epubs.iltanet.org/i/1097368-spring-2019/14?.
35. *See* Tom Kelley and David Kelley, *Creative Confidence: Unleashing the Creative Potential within Us All* (2015).
36. "Our minds are generally lazy and like to get rid of problems as quickly as possible, so they surround first ideas with a lot of positive chemicals to make us 'fall in love' with them. Most often, our first solutions are pretty average and not very creative. Humans have a tendency to suggest the obvious first. Learning to use great ideation tools helps you overcome this bias."
37. *See* Tom Kelley and David Kelley, "Reclaim Your Creative Confidence", *Harvard Business Review* (December 2012), available at https://hbr.org/2012/12/reclaim-your-creative-confidence; *see also supra* note 36.
38. Hagan, *supra* note 3, at www.lawbydesign.co/en/design-mindsets/.
39. Taylor Pearson describes this as the product/market/founder fit framework for deciding what to focus on. Taylor Pearson, *The Paint Drop Method for*

Figuring Out What To Do with Your Life (and Becoming the Best in the World At It), https://taylorpearson.me/what-should-i-do-with-my-life/.

40. Here is a curated list of the top 49: https://bookauthority.org/books/best-prototyping-books. Amani recommends Jake Knapp, John Zeratsky, Braden Kowitz, *Sprint: How to Solve Big Problems and Test New Ideas in Just Five Days* (2016) for an approachable read on how to kick-start the design thinking process (from discovery to prototyping) with a team in just a week.
41. *See* www.futurelawpractice.org/.
42. Burnett and Evans, *supra* note 5, at 81.
43. Stuart R. Levine, *Outperform with a Growth Mindset Culture*, Forbes (26 February 2019), www.forbes.com/sites/forbesinsights/2019/02/26/outperform-with-a-growth-mindset-culture/#7242726e3c2c.
44. The hidden job market includes jobs which are never posted or posted as a formality after a hire has already been identified, and is estimated to account for a majority of hiring decisions. *See, e.g.*, Lauren Weber and Leslie Kwoh, "Beware the Phantom Job Listing", *Wall Street Journal* (8 January 2013), available at www.wsj.com/articles/SB10001424127887323706704578229661268628432.
45. References to networking on social media may surprise you. However, it has multiple benefits. Social media opens up national (and even international) communities for knowledge sharing and engagement. It is possible to have interactions and conversations with executive level professionals that you would otherwise have a hard time meeting. Similarly, social media offers accessible platforms on which to build a personal brand and develop name recognition in your desired field. A number of Amani's law school colleagues found jobs or made connections that led to jobs on Twitter, and when hiring Amani has successfully used Twitter to advertise postings to relevant candidate pools.
46. *See* 2019 State of the Industry Survey, Corporate Legal Operations Consortium, 13 (July 2019), available at https://cloc.org/wp-content/uploads/2019/07/2019-State-of-the-Industry-FINAL.pdf ("Legal Operations professionals are accounting for a larger portion of their departments as the function grows in scope and new roles are added.").
47. *See, e.g.*, Melody Wilding, *The Five Types of Impostor Syndrome and How to Beat Them*, Fast Company (18 May 2017), available at https://www.fastcompany.com/40421352/the-five-types-of-impostor-syndrome-and-how-to-beat-them.
48. Dr. Seuss, *Happy Birthday to You!* (1959).
49. Burnett and Evans, *supra* note 5, at 218.
50. *See* Meredith Somers, *A Guide to Intrapreneurship*, Ideas Made to Matter, MIT Sloan School of Management (21 June 2018), https://mitsloan.mit.edu/ideas-made-to-matter/a-guide-to-intrapreneurship
51. See Angela Lee Duckworth's research on grit. https://angeladuckworth.com/research/
52. Burnett and Evans, *supra* note 5, at xv.

Chapter 12: Quick and dirty – tactics for leveraging design thinking in your daily work

By Andy Peterson and Kate White, Design Build Legal

Introduction

We first discovered the power of design thinking back in 2012. Our employer at the time, the Seattle-based law firm Davis Wright Tremaine, was just beginning its innovation journey, and we tasked ourselves with reaching out to innovative clients outside the legal industry. We met with an angel investor who talked about the need to design user-centered products. "Make your product as easy as possible to get in the door," he said. "Think of the entry point as the tip of a needle. Hopefully, once your customers are using it, they won't want to stop." We spoke with a tech CEO who talked about fixed fees, and the need for pricing for value, not hours. "Lawyers will never get truly rich on the billable hour," he said, "because hours are finite." "Well," we replied, "many of them are doing... pretty well."

Fortuitously, we were introduced to Ben Grossman-Kahn, who at the time headed up the Innovation Lab at Nordstrom, a client of the firm. This led to us being invited to take part in one of Nordstrom's Innovation Bootcamps, where about 50 Nordstrom employees would put design thinking into action. Our challenge – to create the "Nordstrom Rack of the future". Over two days, we held empathy interviews with Nordstrom customers, defined a problem statement, iterated on solutions, and took our prototypes out to the streets of Capitol Hill to test them with shoppers. Based on that user feedback, we worked to revise our prototypes based on the needs of customers, and took *those* prototypes back out to test. Ideate. Prototype. Test. Again and again.

After two full days of design thinking, we were exhausted. But we were blown away by how rapidly we could reimagine the customer experience, and actually start putting changes into place. Coming out of the boot camp, we were driven to figure out how we could apply design thinking in legal. We had to stretch our minds a bit to think about how we could use the same techniques to reimagine professional services, rather than products. How would we use design thinking to innovate for clients, when they so rarely come to our physical space? And the firm (at the time) wasn't in the business of developing products, for which feature ideas can be sourced and applied to new versions.

All these years later, we have had scores of successes, bringing design thinking into the delivery of legal services, both as founding members of DWT De Novo, the innovation arm of Davis Wright, and as the co-founders of Design Build Legal, where we infuse design thinking into virtually everything we do. And there are lots of folks trying to bring design thinking to legal, including consultants coming in from other industries.

But those outsiders are learning what readers of this book know well – legal is different. Wouldn't it be great if you could grab 20 people from your office, have them block their calendars for three days, bring in your key clients, and do a full-on design thinking workshop to create the next great firm–client product? Of course! But you work in legal, where that sort of thing is particularly difficult to pull off. So, does that mean that design thinking is off the table?

Luckily, no! There are practical ways to infuse your daily work with aspects of design thinking. This chapter will show you how to turn around that group meeting that always devolves into a complaint session; solve a challenge by expanding the number of voices in the room; gain buy-in from leadership around making new investments; and create stronger relationships between your firm and your clients.

One final note before we begin. For simplicity, we wrote this chapter with a law firm audience in mind. But many of these stories – and all of these tactics – apply to the in-house experience as well. If you're an in-house counsel or legal operations professional, just replace "firm" with "department", and view the advice through your lens.

Rapid ideation – turning challenges into solutions

Imagine a common scenario – you're in a team meeting, discussing a problem you've discussed several times before. Your colleague says, "I received an email from XYZ client earlier today. The GC is feeling caught off-guard by our most recent bill. Said he expected it to be half the amount it is. I guess we need to write off a bunch of time again."

All too often, we're so busy that we tend to just nod our heads "yes" to this type of problem – agree to the quick fix, the write-off – and move on. Design thinking challenges us to think differently about how we solve problems. It shifts our mindset. Rather than defaulting to existing systems or processes, it challenges us to invent new ones.

What if this team took 15 minutes to ask the question: how might we prevent clients from feeling caught off guard by our bills after we've already completed the work? By framing the problem with a "How might we?" statement, you open up the possibility for people to think beyond the ways in which things are currently done. Now it's time to get out the post-its and sharpies, and come up with as many ideas as you can in five minutes, or three minutes. In fact, you'd be surprised how many ideas people can come up with in as little as 60 seconds using this method.

"Ad hoc ideating," if you will, is a great practice to instill in team meetings. Here's what it might look like:

> *"I agree that we'll probably have to write some time off, but let's spend a few minutes in today's meeting ideating on how we might prevent this and other clients from feeling caught off guard by our bills in the future. There are post-Its and sharpies on the table. Let's start at this end of the room and work our way around, with each person saying, and then headlining their idea, on a post-it. I'll grab them all at the end of the meeting and set up a bit more time with a smaller group to refine the ideas and determine next steps toward designing something that might solve this."*

In most companies, it wouldn't be uncommon for everyone to stand up at a white table and slap their post-it ideas up on the board. But, if your law firm's conference room (or culture) isn't feeling conducive to this, simply staying seated and noting ideas on post-its is a big step forward.

Once you're back at your office with the collection of ideas, you can organize them on the wall or a white board, placing them in categories. Then, at the next meeting, you could bring a few of the best ideas, further refined, back to the group to discuss, and perhaps even invest in developing. You could also bring together a smaller group, outside of the team meeting structure, that you think would be engaged in designing something new, working together to come up with a prototype that you can bring back to the larger group or to firm leadership.

Rather than defaulting to the current system – complain, give up, give in, brace for the problem to come up again – you're focusing the team's energy towards a solution.

Cross-functional teams – expanding the diversity of voices in the room

Most law firms these days will tout that they have teams that are centered around key engagements with strategic clients. However, these "client teams" are often more marketing than material – meeting infrequently, rarely engaging directly with the client, and focused entirely on making sure that "the right hand knows what the left hand is doing" in order to minimize "client service mistakes". These teams are too infrequently focused on how to best serve the client – solving their legal problems, sure, but also tackling the client's business and operational challenges. It is here that another key lesson from design thinking – one you can apply every day – comes into view: the value of diverse teams when it comes to problem-solving.

When a team comes together to solve any challenge, the individuals bring their own perspectives and experiences to the table. A plumber sees a challenge differently than a banker; a priest will look at a problem in a way that a weightlifter may not. Each will suggest solutions based on their own opinions and experiences, and what they've seen work in the past. Five weightlifters will probably come up with the same types of solutions. Five priests will probably do the same. And hey, the conclusions reached in silos by these groups of like-minded individuals may work. They may solve the problem. But by pairing a priest and weightlifter, their diverse perspectives give them a *greater* chance at a *better* solution.

It's the same inside your law firm. Five partners will have similar knowledge and experience, and will therefore look to solve a challenge in generally the same way. Even a mix of partners from different practice groups will look at things similarly, because at the end of the day, an IP partner and an M&A partner are still law firm partners. "So, should we throw in an associate?" I mean, sure. Now you've added a younger, possibly more tech-savvy, lawyer, so that's better. But if you really want to gain the benefit of "cross-functional teams" in solving client challenges, you should be thinking beyond the core timekeepers on the client's matters.

Who is the accounting person that handles billing on the client? Their understanding of the numbers, and metrics like profitability, would come in handy.

Next, pull in an IT person. Even if they aren't coders per se, and are primarily tasked with "keeping the lights on" at the firm, their technical perspective probably dwarfs that of your lawyers. (No offense.)

If your firm has an LPM team, bring a project manager to the table. They bring their own perspective, along with something – a best practice, a lesson learned, even a "trick" or two – from every project they've worked on beforehand.

Who is the marketing or business development person who supports the primary practice group? They probably have a business or journalism degree, and their experience in communicating value, and marketing your practice, will be a useful addition to the team. Not to mention, in our experience, marketing has the broadest view across the firm of any administrative department. They don't just keep the website humming, or collate your RFP materials. They are tasked with taking the things that are happening across the firm – wins, pitches, events, new clients – and communicating those stories internally and externally. If an idea has been born, lived, succeeded, or died, anywhere across your offices, there's a good chance a marketing person worked on it or heard about it, and can connect you with the person who championed it and learned from the experience.

Finally – and these folks are too often overlooked – include a legal assistant or other admin person on the team. Legal assistants typically staff a number of lawyers at once, so they tend to be more pragmatic than their lawyers. They don't get bogged down in the minutiae, and they don't overanalyze. We can't tell you how many times we have seen a tough problem – even a legal problem – solved in part thanks to the perspective of a legal assistant, whose advice began with "Why don't you just do (X)?"

There are a couple additional benefits of creating these truly cross-functional teams with administrative staff alongside the lawyers. One big one is that, once the team comes up with the solution, the actual hard work begins – the execution. You're going to want some "doers" who can drive the execution forward, and having someone who can go back to IT or marketing or accounting on the team's behalf can be invaluable. Also, remember that associate you "threw in" earlier? They are less likely to be intimidated by a room full of partners – if the room isn't just full of partners.

So, leverage the design thinking lesson of cross-functional teams. Particularly when the client challenge is a sticky one. Otherwise… well, you might need that priest.

Prototyping and testing – making investments that you know will hit the mark

Lawyer: "Good morning. I would like $50,000 for a new technology."
CFO: "Wow, that's a lot of money."
Lawyer: "Yes, but it's really going to help our clients."
CFO: "Oh, OK, which ones?"
Lawyer: "Well this could help literally hundreds of our clients."
CFO: "OK, but again, which clients?"
Lawyer: "Important Client #1 and Strategic Client #2, to start."

CFO: "OK, so you've been talking with them?"
Lawyer: "Well, I mean, they told me they had a problem, and I believe this technology would solve it."
CFO: "But what if it can't?"
Lawyer: " … "
CFO: "Hello?"

Do you ever see those press releases from law firms, announcing that they are bringing on "Fancy New Technology X" because #innovation and #clients? How often do you see a second press release showing how they are using the tool to directly benefit clients? Sorry to be cynical here, but the answer is "not often enough". This is because firms too often worry about (a) the cost of the technology, (b) how it will integrate with their other tools, and (c) how it will affect the people inside the firm (e.g. "Will it make my job harder?"). It's almost *assumed* that the technology will benefit the client downstream, if we can *just* make sure it works for the firm. That assumption, like all assumptions, is dangerous.

Let's say that your empathy interview sourced a challenge inside the client's business around managing contracts. (A common theme, these days.) And then let's say that your cross-functional team thought up a good idea – a dashboard that lists all the contracts, including some metadata about each, with a link to view the actual contract. Now, there are $50,000 technologies out there that do this, out of the box. You could buy one! Today! But how do you know that it will really solve the client's needs? And if it does, how do you know that it can scale and broaden, if (when) the client says, "I wish it could do (X)"?

Design thinking teaches us about the power of prototyping and testing in order to make sure a solution will hit its target. Once we've completed the ideation part of design thinking – throwing out our 20 or 50 or 100 ideas, thoughts that build on one another, and then selecting the best – design thinking tells us to go ahead and just build it.

So, we get out a big piece of paper, and we draw. Here's what the front end looks like: the list of contracts, and the metadata we want to show up-front – the expiration date of the contract, the amount of money involved, and whether it has an auto-renewal clause or needs to be renegotiated. Here are some of the metrics we will report out: cycle times, volume by department, most-negotiated clauses. Pen and paper. It's not fancy, but pretty soon, we have ourselves something we can share with the client for feedback: a prototype.

Now, this is something that lawyers are not great at – taking something to a client before it's "done" – and we get that. There is a reason firms have massive malpractice insurance policies. Lawyers are trained to provide The One Best Answer. Or, if necessary, A Range Of Answers With Caveats.

But when it comes to solving a client's business or operational challenge, there is no One Best Answer. What there often is, is a problem that may just barely touch on legal analysis at all. For example, yes, there is a legal aspect to contracting. But go back to your empathy interview – the issue the client raised was more about *managing* the contracts than it was about risk mitigation. So, the danger is relatively low.

Take the prototype to the client and walk them through it. *Is this the metadata you would want to see front and center?* Ask what else would they would want to capture. *Are these the metrics that would move the needle for you?* Find out who would interact with a tool like this, and how they would do so. *What other features would make your job easier?* Get their thoughts on what's missing, and what's extraneous.

If you're lucky, you will get to do a couple rounds of prototyping and testing. And, in the end, you will have come up with a solution that incorporates actual user feedback. You can take that prototype out to the market to see the available options – what you can buy, or what you might build – and how closely those options come to the target. Furthermore, because you have engaged the client in the process, they are bought in; they can see how your investment would help them, and they may even be excited about it. In this instance, your firm is not just a legal advisor, but a true business partner. And isn't that the goal?

And this takes us back to that conversation with the CFO. Instead of asking for an investment that *might* hit the mark for *some* clients, you've got a specific solution, informed by the feedback of potential users, and identified in partnership with a client who can see how it would solve a key challenge. The likelihood of getting that money has gone up exponentially. As have the chances you get to send that second press release.

Empathy interviews – creating stronger firm–client relationships

Developing empathy for your user is the first step in the design thinking process. To do this, we must develop the ability to see the world through other people's eyes, something we can only do by putting aside our preconceived notions, being humble, and working to understand the needs of others.

We would argue that the practice of developing empathy for your customer or client is the most impactful component of the design thinking process. Yet, all too often, we see law firms skip this step

– designing what they *think* clients might want, leaving their end users completely out of the design process, as in the scenario described above. Unfortunately, this often leads to investments in ideas or products that don't actually solve clients' problems, or products that they're not willing to pay for, or products that don't fit within the context of their environments.

For years, we have conducted what we call "client insights interviews" on behalf of firms of all sizes. These conversations are purposefully distinct from those involved in more traditional client feedback interviews, which are often centered around the firm's performance. Client insights interviews are focused exclusively on the client contact. How is he or she measured? What are the operational challenges that his or her department is struggling to solve? What does the in-house counsel find frustrating about managing outside counsel? Where is he or she looking to provide reporting to the GC or the C Suite that he or she isn't currently able? These questions are focused on one thing – developing empathy for clients, in the hopes that you might help them solve problems.

Once you've uncovered these client insights, you and your firm have an opportunity to start thinking – and designing – like the Big Four – developing "integrated solutions" to clients' problems, rather than solving for one-off discrete legal issues.

While these empathy-building discussions lend themselves well to uncovering opportunities to solve client challenges and make clients' lives easier, another key place to apply design thinking is at the start of a *new* relationship.

We had the pleasure of supporting a firm in designing, from scratch, the firm's relationship with a new client, for which the firm would be a first-time preferred provider. We led a design discussion with three of the in-house counsel with whom the firm would be supporting. We sat in a room with a large white board, and we framed the challenge, "How might we…?"

From there, we ideated on ways in which the firm could provide the in-house team with greater transparency into matters; greater predictability around legal bills and budgets; and a consistent best-practices work product for one of the practice areas in which it would be working. We also focused on things like client communication preferences; establishing service level agreements; developing a consistent two-way feedback loop; and how we might leverage the other professionals at the law firm to help the client apply data analysis and visualization to proactively identify risk and trends. At the end of this half-day session with members of the in-house team, we had a blueprint for a firm–client relationship that considered the client's goals, preferences, and expectations. We also had clients that were blown away with the firm's investment of time, up-front (and off-the-clock), to get the relationship right from the beginning.

Now, as you can imagine, the greater challenge in this exercise was seeing that the firm actually executed on this vision. We can tell you that, indeed, it did. Some of that follow-through can be credited to the firm implementing a client account management program – a topic for a different chapter, in a different book.

Conclusion

Design thinking is a powerful methodology for creating valuable firm–client relationships. If you can get key members of the firm and client together for a full day to work through the entire design thinking process, guided by someone who really knows what they're doing, you will no doubt create a stronger bond between the two teams, in addition to identifying possible solutions to mitigate client challenges.

But even if you can't get the day, or the teams together in person, there are a number of ways to apply the key principles of design thinking to your daily work. The next time you find that the old way of doing things just isn't working, you now have the tools to break through.

Chapter 13: Design thinking mindsets that are counter-intuitive for lawyers

By Mark Beese, President, Leadership for Lawyers llc

One of the reasons design thinking has been slow to catch hold in legal is that some of the underlying mindsets are counter-intuitive for lawyers. It is not that lawyers can't embrace and practice these mindsets. Rather, their training, incentives, and environment have often encouraged the opposite attitude or behavior that is needed to innovate in this way. I facilitate Design Thinking for Legal© workshops for lawyers, legal professionals, and legal operations leaders in law firms and legal departments. The workshops consist of an introduction to the concept of design thinking in the legal environment, mindsets and tools for the process, and an intense hackathon where participants learn the entire process by doing it step-by-step. Here are a few examples, and some insights on how to change mindsets.

Stanford's d.School (Hasso Plattner Institute of Design at Stanford – where design thinking originated) has a list of six mindsets that are supportive of the design thinking process:

1. Human centered;
2. Radical collaboration;
3. Show, not just tell;
4. Prototype;
5. Bias towards action; and
6. Trusting the design thinking process.

Let's take a look at each of these mindsets in the context of the legal environment.

Human centered

We design for the benefit of people, who have preferences, emotions, and insights that may not be apparently rational to legal professionals. Starting in law school, lawyers are taught policies and procedures. Associates and young professions are mentored to follow checklists and processes that are long established in order to get it "right". Work quality, accuracy, and avoiding all mistakes are paramount to how lawyers are evaluated.

Innovation through design thinking doesn't negate these standards, but it does emphasize another facet of delivering legal service. Is the client delighted? Is this process the most efficient? How can we redesign the process to reduce inefficiencies and frustration while maintaining high work quality standards? How can we best leverage technology to reduce time-intensive (i.e. boring and duplicitous) tasks? How might we redesign our work systems to engage and challenge young professionals who have different expectations of professional life than those 50 years ago?

Design thinking requires legal designers (lawyers, legal operations leaders, law firm leaders, who are focused on innovation and client service) to "see with new eyes" and look for ways to improve the experience for people. To be more human-centered, we need to engage in dialogue and improve our observation skills to see beyond our preconceptions and be open to changing our view of reality.

One doesn't have to look far to find problems to solve. For example:

- Ask clients what irritates them the most about how legal work is done in their area of expertise. Where is there a waste of time, money, or resources? What resource, tool, or feature would make their life easier? What part of the process doesn't make sense to them? If they had a magic wand to fix one thing to make their work life easier, what would that be?
- Ask associates about what drives them crazy about working in the firm or department. Where do they waste the most energy? What systems or processes baffle them? What makes them want to pack it up and go into a different career?
- Ask law firm staff members their ideas on how to improve client service and value.
- Ask someone outside of the legal ecosystem how their company or industry is changing how they serve clients, streamline processes, or manage their business. This can be a source of ideas and inspiration.

- Observe behaviors of the people around you and ask, "Why are they doing what they are doing? What irritates them? Is there a problem we can solve here? What "wows" them? Is there a lesson we can apply elsewhere here?"

Radical collaboration

Design thinking requires a high level of collaboration between legal designers, users, outside experts, and other stakeholders. However, many lawyers in law firms and legal departments often operate in silos or within small, protected groups. Design thinking requires us to get out of our comfort zone and work with outside experts, clients (both in legal departments and in operating units), and other legal professionals to develop innovative solutions to wicked problems. The diversity of these collaborative groups often are the "magic" that leads to true innovation.

When leading an innovation initiative, ask yourself, "What perspectives might we be missing? Who might have an insight on this problem that is different than mine?" Be curious. Ask questions. Expand your network. This mindset is critical in each phase of the design thinking process. Consider how you will engage diverse perspectives when gathering information, crafting the design problem/point of view, brainstorming ideas, selecting ideas for prototyping, prototype development and testing. Can you see how involving users, outside experts, colleagues, and other stakeholders could be beneficial at each stage?

Try practicing collaboration as a daily habit. Rather than doing something just by yourself, how could you invite someone else on a project and share the work (and the credit)? Be aware of what contributions other people bring to a project and check your negative reactions to collaboration. What you might initially see as a threat might not be in reality. Try to understand that collaboration might take a little longer and require some diplomacy, but in the end the contributions and insights of others will make the innovation initiative more successful.

Show, not just tell

Lawyers love words. Lawyers are taught to write and speak clearly from our first law school class and embark on a lifelong journey to improve these skills. Drawing pictures, diagrams, process maps, journey maps, and Gantt charts are not natural for most attorneys. Actually building a physical prototype can be even more challenging. The design thinking process works best when we communicate our ideas with both words and images. These visual representations often reveal insights, ideas, and solutions that well-chosen words might conceal.

Try thinking in pictures and processes more frequently. Just for kicks, practice drawing process maps of activities that you are involved in. What would a process map of "getting ready for work" look like? Try drawing it out. Then dig deeper and ask yourself if you have missed any steps. Where are the opportunities to improve this process? Try mapping out a process at work, like preparing a contract. Dig deeper. What are the opportunities for process improvement? Try mapping a process that affects you or others at work, like a new attorney onboarding process or implementation of a new policy. Dig deeper. What are the opportunities for improvement?

Journey maps are process maps on steroids. With a journey map, we try to better understand a person's experience with the process to provide insight into the problem we're trying to solve. Try taking one of the process maps you've designed and, below it, ask questions like, "What was I feeling at this stage? Was it energizing or did it sap me of energy? Did I get a good result, or was it mediocre at best? What are the risk factors at this stage?" Add factors that are most relevant to the user's (you or someone else) experience.

Take some time to practice sketching ideas. You won't be graded on your artistic talent. I promise. Rather, practice communicating in more of a visual medium to communicate your ideas. Try adapting your presentations to use more images and diagrams. Practice communicating visually.

Prototype

A critical element of design thinking is developing prototypes for empathy (learning) and for testing (feasibility). It is tempting to skip over this phase and go right to a final solution, but when we do that, we miss an important opportunity to learn from the user's reaction to the idea.

Prototyping is challenging for some attorneys because it goes against their grain of only showing work product that is 100 percent perfect. Showing an idea that is half-baked in order to get feedback shows that we might not get it right the first time. In fact, we never do. This try-learn-fix-improve cycle is natural when developing software or consumer products, but it is often a challenge to those of us in the legal world. We need to embrace the reality that to innovate is to learn from failure. By prototyping early and frequently, we can save effort and money and develop a more effective solution in the end.

Prototyping – indeed, engaging in innovation itself – requires the legal designer to be more comfortable saying, "Let's try this on a small scale, or with one client, or one group and see what we learn from it". Try experimenting more. It may mean developing a small community of trial users or groups – those who might be more naturally inclined to experiment with you and give you structured and valuable feedback.

Product designers often use a "shop" to make physical representations of a product for prototyping. Software designers will develop a prototype and recruit "early adopters" for beta testing. Legal designers would benefit from creating a formal or informal group of lawyers, users, experts, and staff that have diverse skills in process design, graphic design, project management, financial analysis, legal operations, technology and automation, and human resources/professional development. Such a prototyping team could collaborate to design new legal or operational processes, test the prototype, and analyze the results.

On a personal level, if you struggle with the concept of prototyping, try experimenting by doing a few things differently, and asking others for feedback. Pick a personal design project, develop a few different ways of solving a problem, and engage others to evaluate each solution. Practice prototyping.

Bias towards action

This design thinking mindset encourages designers to focus more on action – listening, analyzing, focusing, brainstorming, prototyping, evaluating, prototyping more, testing, and doing it all over again. Not that there is anything wrong with thinking and talking, but action around a prototype (even if that prototype is a process map or test program) reveals more than thinking what might happen. Sometimes we're wrong about how we think users might react to an idea. We have a tendency to talk ourselves out of a truly innovative idea because we don't think it would fly, even before we test it.

Legal designers need to be aware of the gravitational force to over analyze and "group-think" solutions to death. Designers need to create a sense of urgency and focus on activating the next step in the process. Otherwise the innovation team will be at risk of analysis paralysis.

Legal designers might want to consider taking management tips from the software or manufacturing design industries, such as using "design sprints" to quickly move through a design iteration cycle, creating artificial deadlines if necessary. This does not mean that a firm or legal department should rush a new process improvement or innovation initiative to launch. Rather, it means creating a momentum of discrete tasks that contribute to the design process to prevent the initiative from getting stalled or people losing interest. Designers need to ask, "What's next? What are the outcomes or feedback we expect from this task? What is next after that?"

Project management tools such as project schedules, Gantt charts, sub-team assignments, and quick check-in meetings can help a team stay focused on action.

Trusting the design process

The design thinking process is not one that works well if you skip or skimp on a step. Legal designers need to respect and trust the process and mindsets to deliver an innovative result. If you find that your design team is not coming up with true innovation, it is probably because you didn't trust the process.

This happens all the time. A design team is energized by the brainstorming phase, and identifies two or three brilliant ideas to test. But rather than develop prototypes and go through the arduous task of testing, getting feedback, revising and combining the prototypes, and doing it all over again, the team (or team leader) goes right to production. "Why can't we just do this tomorrow? Bias towards action, right? Let's just do it. Everyone will love it!" Until they don't, because by skipping the iterative feedback and revise step, you've missed critical information that can determine the full potential of the innovation.

Trust the process. Respect each step. Challenge yourself and your team on how you can get the most out of each mindset and step. Don't belabor the process, but understand that the design thinking process is self-correcting, human-centered, creative, authentic, collaborative, diverse and relies on a lot of moving parts that leads to an innovative solution that garners broad acceptance.

The process usually leads to an innovative solution that truly delights the user or client. By being collaborative and involving many diverse stakeholders, it helps you prepare your script for a successful launch. The legal designer knows from prior feedback what the distractors will say and understand who they need to win over to gain support for the initiative. Skip a step or two, and your launch strategy may be flawed.

Don't give up

Here's a bonus mindset. *Don't give up.* Innovation in the legal world is challenging for many reasons. We operate on a precedence system, which by natures assumes that somebody has done it before. Innovation isn't like that. Lawyers by nature are more risk-adverse and change-conservative than any other profession. That's probably a good thing, given that we help people and companies act according to the law, but it is a challenge when it comes to being innovative.

Still, our market and profession is changing rapidly. Some might call it a disruptive market environment with new entrants ("alternative service providers"), new competitors (Big 4 Accounting firms and others), new technology (AI and automation, new models (virtual law firms), and increasingly intense client pressure to lower costs, improve service and be more strategic (can't just choose two – you need all three). Innovation is an imperative.

Legal designers need to be relentless evangelists of design thinking. Trust the process. Show early successes. Elevate successful innovation initiatives. Illustrate how early and limited failures led to increased awareness and better solutions in the end. Legal designers are responsible for leading change in their organizations that will eventually change the culture to be more open-minded, experimental, client-focused, technology-savvy, employee-engaged and ultimately a better place to work.

Chapter 14: Practical approaches for making service design work in a global law firm

By Alex Smith, global product lead, iManage RAVN

The journey to this service design perspective

Let's differentiate design thinking from service design. Design thinking has a DNA that has bled into service design, but service design is an evolution of both user experience and user centric design. My journey into this came through a product management lens, and was therefore tied to the user experience around digital experience design. I love design thinking methodology, have been trained on it and use elements of it, but it's not where my origins lie. In fact, I didn't hear about design thinking until 2015 when I was already a decade down a practical journey of working in a customer-led team at LexisNexis.

Regardless of what your journey is to service design, or design thinking, what's most important is putting the customer first and dedicating time to understanding the customer, getting to know them and listening. Ultimately, this is the core of the entire methodology.

Service design is more than a hackathon or a "design sprint". It's immersive, it entails being out with the users, championing tough messages back to the business. It's showing results that move a project, business, or legal aid initiative forward. Most importantly, the voice of the user cuts through the noise of internal HIPPOs (**H**ighest (**I**ncome) **P**aid **P**erson's **O**pinion) in any organization. Often the brutal feedback on your service or product is a catalyst to real change. That feedback is a key guide to how to evolve and change legal services. Leaving behind the ego and listening to the voice of client is at the heart of this.

During my time in product management at LexisNexis as a product manager and new product lead I got to work closely with the user experience team on user projects around how lawyers interface with information and know-how. The projects were all deep dives into how lawyers mentally approached problems but also in the context of where they started and what they were doing. Some examples of these projects give an idea of the scale of research that goes into service design at scale.

- **Search intent** – we interviewed c. 50 lawyers around their approach to search to understand the intent of users when approaching a search box to help improve the experience of search. This involved delving into wider processes and tasks they were doing as well as the clues given by clients or senior lawyers as to what to look for.
- A two-year **customer discovery program** that our team ran, interviewing lawyers on what they did in their work, mapping their days, examining the systems they work in and the processes they work within (and mapping these). I covered in-house legal and later the judiciary. The open interview approach challenged many assumptions around customer research, the openness of participants to talk about their roles (our senior leadership assumed this wasn't possible) and how to engage people around discussing their roles, testing concepts and iterating concept and product designs.
- A nine-week **Design Sprint process** (nine consecutive one-week design sprints) to rapidly prototype and iterate the product vision (that had been lost from user needs and discovery due to internal stakeholder "opinion") for the UK legal market. This included rapid user testing of iterative outputs and a full user study of their reaction to final outputs and options. Working at scale in design sprints and reflecting weekly on what worked and throwing out what didn't was eye-opening due to their ability to move so fast if you dedicated full-time people and resources.

Why reflect on these experiences? First, lessons learnt and how the approach to user-centric design has evolved from interface design into complete user journeys and then into the service design approach. Second as a precursor to how to apply this to the current law firm, in-house legal or NewLaw environment where there is less acceptance of this approach to research. The product management experience at LexisNexis was of user research at scale, working with professional product and UX people, designing research from existing product issues or looking at new markets. Research would take several months, designed by phases, insight from iterative phases, new phases of research (or starting back from scratch), designs prototyped, one-way mirror user testing, and global testing across countries where product features were shared (with jurisdictional lawyer differences). Welcome to joining a law firm and a world of difference … and of opportunities. Law firms and alternative legal service providers are a long way from the service design at the scale of banks and the industries they serve.

Experience of going into a law firm with a product approach

In 2016, I moved from Lexis Nexis to head up the Innovation Hub program at Reed Smith. At that time, all the hype around legal technology was about artificial intelligence, new technologies, and blockchains. It was clear to me that everyone was missing the key first stage. No one was asking the critical question: what problem are we trying to solve? It was equally obvious from talking to the firm's clients that any innovation initiative had to be grounded in real user needs and impact on how legal services are delivered. The firm had a great attitude to collaboration with its clients, and partnering to develop solutions, but the innovation hub was a new initiative. Having come from a product and UX background you want to take the learned best practices and implement them, but I had no resources, and I was facing a skeptical audience of lawyers to whom this was brand new. Where to begin?

Smuggler mentality

Time could have been spent trying to win over lawyers to an "alien" methodology and build the case for a program around service design and user experience. Or that time could be spent actually doing the basics and getting early wins into the firm.

This low key approach is one I call "innovation smuggling". Having an innovation smuggler mentality allowed me to use design thinking approaches at every opportunity, from basic meetings to change projects to process improvement sessions without anyone realizing it was happening. Compared to existing approaches, the wins that could be gained almost immediately in terms of better, more collaborative outcomes were huge. Implementing the smuggler mentality meant that even though people didn't know how we were doing it, we were getting deeper feedback from sessions by hearing all voices in the room, listening for nuance in what people say, and gathering real insight. Explaining after a success how it was achieved is more powerful than trying to explain something foreign upfront to get permission.

Getting the voice of the customer (client)

Law firms (and law companies) thrive off the power of "what clients said" – it's a form of capital and power. The issue for teams that want to take a user-centric approach is that lawyers preciously guard their client relationships. Many knowledge management and innovation teams lament the fact that they are not client-facing or allowed time with the clients who are the actual end users of the legal product these teams are building. This structure in firms makes it difficult for the right teams to become user-centric.

In order to get around this obstacle, I recommend several approaches:

1. Find a partner or a small practice group that is being driven by a particular client pressure and work with that small group to show how a closer understanding of customer journey maps and/or processes can change the firm–client dynamic.
2. Leverage your own network to start to get insights from clients on their pain points, working processes, and team drivers. The goal is to start small and gain trust by showing the power of insights that service designers will get from live interactions with clients and in-house end users. Showing lawyers the insights they may not be getting allows teams permission to explore further. Getting good feedback from the clients and delivering insights to the clients feeds back in a virtuous circle. Without the voice of the customer, then service design approaches in law firms are not going to work. But there are other areas to pursue, especially in the business development area.

Find the insight loops in a firm and optimize them

One of the greatest missed opportunities in law firms is the open door they have with their business development activities and events and "client listening programs". Firms should be leveraging the opportunity of the willingness of clients to come to (free) onsite events. In addition to holding lecture-style events, firms should offer working service design sessions aimed at inclusion and outcomes from attendees.

In my experience, these sessions are most effective when they are kept small. People attending are not looking for a "hackathon" but rather a mature sharing of views. Sessions that blend legal and the actual delivery of legal services work particularly well.

Use open questions, active listening, structured questioning, and bold conversations. Connect the dots of the firm's interactions with the client teams. The insight gleaned from interviews and open listening sessions can be game-changing for firms in terms of understanding how clients want their firms to work, client pain points and, above all, undiscovered opportunities. It's also important to remember that mere access to clients is not the biggest issue. Using that access in a collaborative way, and trusting your people (not just your partners) to drive user-centric discovery is what ultimately matters.

Move the process mapping to design thinking

Another major area to "smuggle" in service design is during the process design and redesign exercises that have become fashionable in law firms as they are driven towards tighter pricing models. The process mapping approach of lean six sigma is a short hop to proper user journey mapping approaches in service design. Mapping wider than just the "How do we get the process done?" and including client touch-points and client-side activities leads to an overview of the entire process with real context. Making small adjustments in existing process mapping exercises can lead to some quick wins in those processes that win hearts and minds within the firm's practice groups and, again, can generate good client feedback.

Collaborative projects

The issue with legal innovation remains that there is a push and pull between law firms, alternative new law providers and in-house teams that is not yet collaborative. In-house teams are demanding innovation without defining what they mean by it beyond "cheaper legal services". Law firms are offering innovation in press release fodder. They aren't working together on improving services in actual structured, shared projects. One side expects a pre-wrapped outcome without any work and the other side expects to magically know what the other wants. And hackathon and innovation lab weekends are not enough. The next step for design thinking beyond the initial awareness phase is to actually get into deep projects with real commitment from both sides, agreed phases, using the full service design toolkit, full immersive observation, co-creation, concept creation and testing, and running real user tests. At Reed Smith we had started to run these projects with key clients in a three-phased approach with lawyers from the firm and businesspeople from the clients. Other firms are also doing this. It's hard, requires expertise, engagement, and a belief that the process will deliver outcomes. But if we don't get here as an industry, everything we read about service design in law is just innovation theatre.

Keeping things simple

Whether your firm is playing with the idea of legal design, has done some initial exploration, has a service design "innovation smuggler" in the firm, or is trying to scale design thinking into a firm-wide initiative, here are ten key life lessons from the field. These are designed as principles to extract and use on any occasion, from the smallest interaction with clients, to existing activity, to brand new initiatives.

Remember the core principles of service design (from core service design thinking like the *This Is Service Design Doing* book[1]):

- Human-centered – understand the actual users of your service;
- Collaborative – different stakeholders and users need to be brought together;
- Sequential – think of the stages as a process of service and how they interrelate, don't look at ideas in isolation;
- Iterative – do things in stages, learn from each stage, and course-correct when necessary based on learning;
- Real – change needs to be based on real problems not imaginary ones. Don't retro fit problems to ideas and technology solutions. If it's not real it will fail; and
- Holistic – understand the entire service/process end-to-end, not just in your organization but how that is delivered into your client's business.

Ten life lessons in the field

Service design in law #1 – focus on the user

It may go against instinct, but to make service design work as a methodology in law, the focus has to be on the user. Think about what they are trying to achieve, empathize with them, and understand them as humans. Too often, huge assumptions are made about the user or they are forgotten about entirely in the innovation and change process. Remember that the end user needs to see value in what you sell and what you want to sell in future. If you don't know what the end user wants, don't make assumptions. Instead, go and meet them and understand them. You will also need to advocate for them in project or innovation meetings where others may attempt to elevate their assumptions over your actual user feedback.

TIPS:

1. Get to know the real end user, meet them, map out what they do and what they need.
2. Advocate the end user internally, challenge internal assumptions.

3. **Practical tip:** map the current steps users take in a process you're looking to change. Sit and watch them work at their desk, map out the stages they take, and get them to tell you the most painful parts of the process.

Service design in law #2 – not all lawyers are the same

It has become too common these days to paint all lawyers with the same brush. Broad statements such as "all lawyers hate technology" only reveal your bias or the fact you have read Larry Richard and not interacted with lawyers enough to know that they are people too. In preparation for introducing service design, break down the types of lawyers in your firm or organization. Consider their characteristics, needs, and goals. You can create user personas for these types of lawyers and roles that help your team understand who and what the characteristics are of the people you may be targeting in existing and future change projects.

Personas are made up of categories too, but they are richer categorizations based on personal characteristics such as background, preferences, ways of working, time spent on tasks, areas of pain, and how they interface with other organizations.

TIPS:

1. Start to look for patterns in end users – what matters to them, what do they find painful?
2. Start to look for patterns in your clients' teams - what are their roles, what do they use you for?
3. **Practical tip:** build some basic user persona maps for two role levels in your organization. Interview five people for each, and visualize the difference in each role's work and characteristics.

Service design in law #3 – speak to your users

Too much law firm "research" is based on surveying or surveying via consulting bodies, and it is largely ineffective when it comes to understanding end users. Stop the endless surveying. Instead, undertake qualitative research by actually talking to end users with purpose. Think about what you want to discover. Develop a hypothesis and plan how you will engage with people to discover the answers (or to challenge or reject your original premise). Don't take shortcuts, and remember that one-to-one interviews are the best. Don't be tempted to do the "round table" or a focus group. It's hard, will take a long time, but it works. You have to leave your office and meet people.

A colleague who works for a "data insight" consultancy said a recent qualitative set of open interviews had been so rich and rewarding because people had told her new and different things and been honest and candid.

TIPS:

1. Practice putting users first on internal projects to get comfortable, understand what they want from change projects, and discover the contradictions between project outcomes and user needs.
2. Build a network of in-house lawyers (via friends, social media, alumni, client interactions) to keep listening to what they need and how they work.
3. **Practical tip**: interview returning secondees from clients and build a structured set of questions around ways of working, team environment, and the systems they work in.

Service design in law #4 – just listen

Listen to different views and actively listen to those around you. If you're not good at listening you'll miss the opportunity to hear what really matters. I've left meetings where end users have been so open and honest about what is going on in their organization and asked our team, "What did you think of that?" and realized that no one was listening deeply. This equates to missed opportunities. Clients love being listened to. A pragmatic phrase that resonates with me is: "Your opinion, though interesting, is irrelevant". Make sure your team takes note of this.

TIPS:

1. Practice active listening and spend less time talking/broadcasting in meetings.
2. Set up sessions and open questions that allow your client to talk. They talk, you listen.
3. **Practical tip:** run light training on open questions and active listening, and then set a challenge to get insights from "normal" interactions such as dinners, meeting, and coffees. Once you see improved insights from this approach, institute a wider program.

Service design in law #5 – spend time with the problem

A common issue is jumping to solutions or solutions frameworks based on what has worked before. This can lead to missing opportunities to find different ways to solve problems in new and innovative ways. Understanding problems is often overlooked in the desire to assume solutions. However, good service design involves spending as much time as you have in the problem space – understand, explore, be curious, look at the process, and question the premise of the problem. Trying to get more information about the problem, interviewing more end users, and running additional workshops may seem counterintuitive in a fast-paced world, but when you think of the cost in money and time to create solutions, getting right the problem upfront is a cost saving. Generating different solutions to the right problem allows you to plan around short-, medium-, and long-term solutions. Remember, however, that lawyers are trained to get to a solution.

TIPS:

1. Build a framework around the problem. Build clear timelines for exploring the problem.
2. Build approaches with service design techniques that dig deeper into problems and encourage a culture of calling it out when you feel there isn't enough information to move to solutions.
3. **Practical tip:** Run process/user journey sessions where the entire session is about understanding the problem. Make lawyers stay with the problem. Often these sessions lead to reflections on the state of existing processes.

Service design in law #6 – be curious

Be curious and encourage the people you collaborate with to be curious too. Be like the kid in the backseat of the car. Ask why and pull things to pieces, ask bold questions, look at dull systems, observe people working, keep asking why and how. Ask to go on secondments, meet the clients where they live, be bold enough to ask the next level down of questions. Curiosity is a skill you lose as you get older, to fit with conventions and norms.

TIPS:

1. Keep asking questions, learn the "Five Whys"[2] and don't be afraid to use them.
2. Learn to ask great "how" and "why" questions. People will tell you a lot if only you ask them human questions or offer them the chance to share.

3. **Practical tip:** set challenges that allow people to be curious. For example, set a challenge for a trainee changing seats to look at processes as they do so. Get them to ask why there are differences in the ways practice teams work, price work, project manage etc. Get them asking why.

Service design in law #7 – challenge your assumptions

Challenge your assumptions. Even better, leave them at the door and start fresh. By doing so, you'll hear things you didn't know, ask better questions, and find fresh ways to problem-solve. Create exercises and workshops that challenge commonly held assumptions. Often assumptions come from base-level thinking like "Helen used to work here, she'll understand why we do things the way we do", and "I know how their competitor operates, they are all similar". Challenge assumptions by bringing voices of customers into sessions. Get people to write up their assumptions and call them out. Most importantly, challenge your own assumptions first.

TIPS:

1. Make sure you have diverse teams in projects and working sessions, especially lawyer and business services experience sessions.
2. Allow everyone the ability to voice their views. Use service design exercises to get all views out, not just the dominant one.
3. **Practical tip:** run sessions with clients in the room, get them to speak honestly about their work, their needs from your firm, and how they work with their business. Then ask your lawyers in the audience what they heard that was unexpected.

Service design in law #8 – map the user journey

Many firms already have a good working approach to process mapping. Rather than embarking on classic user journey mapping, I would recommend adding human and user experience aspects to existing process mapping work. The challenge of this is doing it in the middle of real work time-pressured organizations. Evidencing wins in the process shows the usefulness of mapping tasks, the roles doing those tasks, and the moments when the processes interact with clients (moments of truth).

Process/user journey mapping sessions get you the human aspects and empathy with different roles on a task or aspect of the process. Getting the coordinator's view on a task can lead to immediate wins through understanding and empathy with different viewpoints on a task.

TIPS:

1. Add to existing process mapping the human, task, and client interaction aspects of the process.
2. Run sessions with clients to map legal processes end-to-end from business ask to in-house team tasks, to bringing on a law firm, to how the legal advice is used back in the business.
3. **Practical tip:** sit with a trainee or associate and get them to talk you through a task/process they do, get them to show you the systems they do it in, then ask them how they feel about the task, how it was given to them, how they found doing it and feedback on how it was done.

Service design in law #9 – ask open questions

The art of asking questions seems obvious but it's amazing how bad people are at doing it. People want measurable answers most of the time, so they ask closed questions – this is why surveying remains the favored insight gathering approach of consultants. Asking the right open questions will drive lots of diverse responses in people's answers, which means the analysis takes a long time. However, the outcome is a richness of insight. Asking open questions means you have to listen and allow the interviewee or workshop participant to open up new avenues of response. Listen to their responses and follow up with targeted open questions like "how" and "why". Ask them to describe their processes and how they work. Listen for rabbit holes and follow that rabbit as unexpected asides are often the most interesting parts of questioning.

TIPS:

1. When creating an interview guide think, can I answer this question with a yes/no answer? If yes, rewrite it.
2. Don't put yourself under time pressure in a user interview. Ask fewer questions and give them more airtime.
3. **Practical tip:** create a basic opening set of questions to make sure you get someone you're talking to open up. Ask them about their role, team structure, their career background (other firms) and then listen to them talk this through.

Service design in law #10 – there are more ways than one to solve a problem
There is never one way to solve a problem if you truly understand that problem and the complexity involved in it. Divergent thinking leads to different perspectives on solutions and options. Service design exercises like "10 plus 10" or approaches to quickly generating 20+ ways to solve a problem force people to think outside the three or four ways they would fall back on. Having multiple teams working independently on the same scenario can highlight that there are a variety of ways to solve a problem or deliver legal services.

TIPS:
1. Get groups to solve a problem or scenario independently and see the different approaches. Play around with the composition of groups.
2. Use idea generation methods like "How might we?" or "10 plus 10" to drive out many options before narrowing in on one or two ideas to work with in detail.
3. **Practical tip:** make space to get all ideas from a room, don't be afraid to get a group to sit in silence for 15 minutes and individually write their ideas down and then get them all up on a wall.

Service design in law
Effective service design requires diversity. Not only should there be cognitive and role diversity, but diversity of background, experiences, and preferably industry/sector. This is challenged in the legal industry, where there is an assumption that the industry comprises only lawyers. In-house lawyers have a greater opportunity in the short-term to bring in business teams with legal operations professionals to drive a diverse culture in legal process and outcomes.

References
1. www.thisisservicedesigndoing.com/
2. https://en.wikipedia.org/wiki/Five_whys

Chapter 15:
The designer's dilemma

By Duncan Hart LLB MBA[1]

It has been difficult to ignore the continued enthusiasm and perceived universal application of what is referred to as "design thinking". This enthusiasm is particularly prevalent amongst those seeking to create innovative and allegedly "disruptive" products, services, and business models for law firms. Its proponents, amongst their many claims, assert that it is not only a source of competitive advantage but sustainable competitive advantage. It is seen as relevant therefore not only in developing new solutions for clients but also improving the creation and delivery of the firm's services.

What is "design thinking"?

Design thinking at its heart is a *process*, a means of identifying, devising, and implementing solutions facing both law firms and their clients. It emphasises, inter alia:

- An "empathic" or "inclusive" approach to ascertaining client needs – understanding not only the "rational" reasons for ascertaining the firm's clients' needs but also their underlying "emotional" drivers;
- The application of a "team-based" focus in identifying and developing appropriate solutions where the "team" includes a diverse range of members and not necessarily "matter experts";
- The development of "rapid out of the box" solutions through ideation, use of graphical tools, and brainstorming; and
- An implementation process focused on the rapid release to market of "prototypes" that are equally rapidly "updated" or improved to reflect customer responses.

What's not to like?

The focus of this chapter is not so much criticism of any one of the key elements that are associated with design thinking. In themselves any one of those elements has much to recommend it. It is more to consider when design thinking:

- May be an inappropriate tool to address the issue at hand compared to more conventional approaches;
- May well be beyond the capability of the firm to effectively implement the process, let alone execute the proposed solutions that might emerge;
- May result in outcomes that conflict with the firm's existing strategic priorities;
- Create unrealistic expectations and impractical "solutions";
- Risks alienating clients;
- Exposes the firm to potential liability; and
- May be promoted for "questionable motives" or to drive an unrelated agenda or as a means of "solving" another issue altogether, e.g. to restore the effectiveness of a poorly performing team.

The "designer's dilemma" therefore is one of urging firms that might be attracted by its appeal to carefully consider the *context* in which such an approach is to be applied; particularly in light of the specific demands, resources, and possible outcomes the process requires. In short, it is to question at the outset that, even if it is considered to be an appropriate approach, can the firm implement the process and carry through its outcomes?

A little history

Design thinking emerged initially from the manufacturing environment but has more recently developed a strong following in the information technology sector and particularly in the start-up environment where, for instance, "user interfaces" have become central to success, particularly on the internet.

Conventionally, a designer in a manufacturing environment did not become involved in the development of a new product until well after the necessary research and development had been undertaken and the product was considered ready for market, save for some stylistic touches that were left to the designers. There was little connection therefore between the product as originally conceived and its final form or functionality, particularly from a customer perspective. Designers, however, began to claim that their "design methodologies" were better suited to understanding and then incorporating client needs into the product development process at a much earlier stage than had been customary.

In other words, rather than initially proceed on the basis of what might turn out to be totally unwarranted assumptions about what clients might eventually need, let alone buy, it was best to develop an understanding as early as possible as to the clients' needs. The next step was to then respond (after appropriate consideration of possible solutions) iteratively to those perceived needs by demonstrating to the client a range of "prototype" solutions before settling on the final form/function of the product concerned. The use of graphical tools and solutions generated from diverse inputs was used widely in creating alternative prototypes, particularly where products were concerned.

Contrast perhaps the development by the British government of the Concorde supersonic airliner in parallel to Boeing's development, at a similar time, of the soon to become all-conquering 747 Jumbo. The key assumption underlying the development of the Concorde was that airline passengers would increasingly demand faster and faster air transport and that the development of a high-speed (twice the speed of sound) airliner would soon conquer the market. Whilst the plane, as developed, was a technological triumph, it failed to address a range of fundamental needs which, had they been considered from a "design" perspective initially, might have led to the development of a completely different type of airliner.

Much of Concorde's commercial failure can be attributed to the fact that it should have been obvious that anything travelling at twice the speed of sound would leave a continuous carpet of window shattering sonic booms over its route. Further, the capacity of the plane was extremely limited (fewer than 100 passengers), and tickets were consequentially very expensive.

Far from an emphasis on speed, however, airlines, and the vast majority of the travelling public, were looking for cheaper travel, rather than faster travel. The limited size of Concorde and its environmental impact meant that its use was confined to a very limited range of routes, which made it unsuitable for the vast majority of airlines that operated over populated areas. Boeing, on the other hand, did a far better job in ascertaining initially what airlines and passengers really wanted. They designed a plane to satisfy those needs – particularly its capacity, its fuel efficiency, and its lack of environmental impact, at least from a noise perspective.

More recently, Apple's meteoric rise has often been attributed to its emphasis on design, both from an aesthetic but also functional point of view, particularly obvious in its initial adoption of its graphical mouse-driven interface for its computers. When initially adopted by Apple, this stood in marked contrast to the then ubiquitous keyboard-driven Microsoft approach. Apple's more user-friendly approach won the day, forcing Microsoft to copy the Apple approach eventually with the launch of Windows.

Both of these examples demonstrate the necessity to establish a strong rapport in the sense of understanding and empathy with the perceived potential market prior to assuming that the status quo or more commonly your "internally" developed solution is actually going to be rewarded with customer enthusiasm.

Empathy... and its limitations

The examples cited above demonstrate the critical importance of ensuring that potential new products and services must in fact satisfy and be responsive to customer needs.[2] This insight[3] has long reflected the approach of the advertising industry and marketing departments generally as an initial step in the development of new products and more recently in rolling out new services to clients.[4] Focus groups, surveys and the now extensive use of comments and reviews in social media, are ubiquitous. In fact, the use of these tools has been so pervasive that it is now becoming extremely difficult to utilise them effectively. "Consumer survey fatigue" is extremely prevalent and any responses actually obtained are often open to considerable doubt due to factors as diverse as hacking and consumer weariness with the process overall. Political polling of potential voting intentions is a case in point of the increasing difficulty and unreliability of such approaches.

There is little new therefore in underlining the importance of gathering, disseminating, and then analysing such information. Developing an "empathic" approach requires encouraging lawyers to "stand in the shoes" of their clients before urging new services or processes upon them. Not always easy to do, particularly where client needs are often expressed in often vague terms such as "no surprises", "value for money", or requiring that their advisors are "easy to deal with". All important issues, but more a starting point in the exercise rather than a means of providing actionable insights.

More practically, particularly in developing new services or competing successfully, is to understand the industry dynamics both at a macro and micro level that impact the client's business on a regular basis.

Demonstrable ignorance of a client's business environment can readily consign the "best" of legal advice or 'new law' services to the rubbish bin and is often cited as a major reason for clients' dissatisfaction with their lawyers.

Considerable ingenuity therefore needs to be exercised in developing one of design thinking's primary requirements, namely "empathy". Lawyers may well do repeat work for large clients on a regular basis and thus be in a position to develop such an empathic approach, but in many practices clients are dealt with in a more transactional fashion with little opportunity to build such empathy.[5] Furthermore, "empathy" must extend well beyond a simple client focus to the wider industry and other macro issues impacting the client and driving those needs, even if the client itself is not aware of, or poorly understands, those issues. Clients often view their own issues through conventional blinkers and are not necessarily the best judges of their best options. Ever "cheaper" legal advice may have universal appeal for clients but a solution that also prevents that particular problem recurring, reduces risks in other areas of their operations, or perhaps helps them grow profitability, should not be overlooked at the altar of "cheapness".

One of the most promising avenues for the application of design thinking would appear therefore to be one where the client and the firm agree to some form of joint exercise to develop a new service or to improve the way in which the firm delivers services to that specific client. Better still, where a firm acts for several clients with similar needs, e.g. a range of local government bodies, the prospects of building the necessary degree of "empathy" in the broader sense and understanding exactly what the client might need (now or in the future) is that much greater.

Coming up with a "solution" – what could possibly go wrong?

Having garnered sufficient information and insight to initially explore potential candidates for your firm's new or improved service, design thinking then requires the design team to brainstorm potential solutions. Needless to say, this requires that those that are invited to take part in such processes:

- Understand how such processes work;
- Hopefully have some real insight to the issues being discussed;
- Can bring the level of expertise as well as the open minded, novel thinking and diverse approach to the exercise; and[6]

- are familiar with brainstorming and the use of graphical and similar team-based tools.

This is no small demand of any team where subject matter experts have an understandable resistance to such processes, particularly if it threatens their status or more specifically the processes or approach they have developed and applied personally over many years. Equally problematically, both at this stage and in garnering sufficient client-centric insights initially, is the tendency of individual lawyers, particularly partners, to claim "ownership" of specific client relationships. Intrusion into "their" client's environment is often viewed with suspicion if not with outright resistance.

Again, this is not to deride the merit of engaging in such a process, but simply to emphasise the potential difficulties in managing such a process in a notoriously time-poor and competitive, rather than collaborative, environment. Such empathetic and team-based collaborative approaches can of course be learned over time, enabling participants to build the necessary expertise to carry out such exercises with increasing levels of skill. One has to be cautious, however, in assuming that the composition of typically existing client or speciality-based teams within law firms is an appropriate test bed upon which to initiate such an approach. Furthermore, it strongly suggests that a good deal of investment in training and leadership would be required initially to underpin this part of the process. What is management's commitment, and how is that being communicated?

Equally obviously, success may be heavily dependent on the complexity of the problem the team is seeking to address. Differing approaches, it is suggested, may be called for in:

- Developing new ways of delivering services; or
- Improving internal law firm efficiencies in comparison to;
- The creation of an entirely new service, strategy or business model or entering an entirely new market.

Implementation – try this on for size

Design thinking calls for the creation of a "prototype" (or series of prototypes), which essentially is a roughed out "good enough" example of the solution the team has extracted from its client insights and brainstorming sessions. The requirement then is that such a prototype be "shipped" as quickly as possible in order to generate client feedback.

This is to quickly enable the prototype to be progressively upgraded to better ensure its eventual success in the market.

In the software environment, Google is perhaps the most notorious user of this approach. Early versions of its software are often released in so-called "beta" state, often to the clear frustration of the market solely for the purposes of utilising the (often) negative feedback for the purposes of rapidly improving or in fact abandoning the original product. In the software environment, immediately deliverable improvements by way of "patches" is technically feasible but one would have to be cautious in assuming a similar process would meet with much enthusiasm from typical law firm clients. Law firms are generally paid to get things right rather than engage in iterative processes that might eventually prove useful. So-called "A/B" testing is well suited for real time feedback in the IT environment, but not so easy, one might conclude, for the average law firm.

Again, the design approach has its place, particularly for instance with regard to improving internal services within the firm and, with some caution, in the way in which the firm interacts with its clients. Clients, particularly of the larger variety, are however often quite dogmatic about the way in which they insist their lawyers interact with them and dictate their preferences accordingly.

Experimentation would no doubt be attractive if the client was convinced that it might reduce costs or improve the speed or effectiveness of the service being offered but less applicable if a prototype solution's benefits are difficult to quickly evaluate. The exercise, however, is obviously fraught with potential negative outcomes that, again, simply emphasise the need for careful implementation of any iterative design driven "prototype" program. A client or a group of clients engaged in a true co-development process would clearly be more understanding and be a more useful target for this type of approach.

Strategic conflict – design your way out of this!

Law firms often more closely resemble conglomerates than individual corporate entities in the sense that it is often difficult to define what the overall strategy of the firm is. It is not unusual to find quite distinct and even competing strategies between teams depending on what markets they service, how they offer their services, and how they view the improvement or development of those services.

Considerable caution is therefore required to ensure that "solutions" developed for one section of the firm's business do not undermine or compromise solutions developed for the firm as a whole or other teams that might be pursuing a more strategically important objective.

All too often, individual teams within firms pay little regard to what strategic priorities the firm may have devised. The upshot is often a disparate group of teams utilising quite different business models that are difficult to service properly and whose priorities have little in common. Design thinking applied against that typical backdrop would require considerable caution to be applied.

It is also difficult to see how design thinking would have practical application in the revision of the firm's existing overall strategy. In particular, whatever the merits might be of developing an empathic view of the firm's clients or potential market, and reviewing options in a diverse team-based environment, it is difficult to see how the firm's strategy could be rolled out in a prototype form and be subject to rapid revision. Such an approach may well have application in a start-up environment as discussed below and in more in detail in my previous publication *Lean Innovation for Lawyers*.[7]

Competing agendas

Careful attention should also be given to the motivation and objectives of those that might promote the use of design thinking within the firm.

Quite often because of its preference for a "team focus" it is seen, particularly by those concerned with the firm's human resources, as a means of building team morale and function. The environment in which the exercise is to take place is often by definition suboptimal. In other words, where open-mindedness, empathy, and non-critical assessment are required, the team concerned often displays few if any of these characteristics and is a poor test bed for the application of design thinking.

Teams within law firms are also conventionally configured around specific clients or particular legal competencies. Again, this form of team is unlikely to have the necessary internal dynamics to apply design thinking processes and, at the very least, a cross-functional team, preferably with client representation and outside members, would be far more appropriate.

Similarly, existing teams are often encouraged to embark on perceived market-driven initiatives, perhaps at the instigation of those principally concerned with marketing within firms. Again, the composition of such conventional teams is unlikely to be a suitable basis for this approach without careful restructuring.

Finally, design thinking initiatives often originate from the firm's own management, which then leaves it to existing team leaders, often very poorly resourced, schooled, or suited, to implement the process. This places considerable onus upon management to ensure that the participants are properly resourced and supported, and understand what and how they are trying to achieve in terms of desired outcomes. Furthermore, team leaders are often either senior members of the firm or are matter experts in particular legal areas. For obvious reasons, such leadership may be quite inappropriate for the task, given the nature of the process that the team is required to undertake.

Where the process is almost certainly best deployed

As mentioned earlier the key elements that comprise the design thinking approach are all tools that law firms could usefully deploy, depending on the context in which they are to be utilised.

The popularity of such an approach can largely be laid at the feet of those promoting the need for innovation and "fresh thinking" in law firms and its strongest advocates (other than consultants) come from the "new law" environment. More often than not, such environments share their structures, ambitions, and funding with start-up, largely technology-focused, entities. These are not entities that are seeking to graft new products or services onto existing frameworks so to speak, but are endeavouring to develop entirely new products or services from what essentially mounts to a blank slate. The design approach that they commonly favour drives or is driven by:

- The selection of its personnel and its preferred team composition;
- Its management style and training priorities;
- Incentives and focus on innovative outcomes; and (most importantly)
- A strategy and business model, which, from the outset, is best suited to the application of design thinking principles.

It is therefore not surprising that established firms that are seeking to either revise their services or devise "new law" products more commonly seek to develop those out of the mainstream of their usual day-to-day operations.

A more common approach emerging now is to see existing firms fund and support such start-ups at arm's length, utilising the inherent strengths of such independent small teams rather than try and replicate the process in-house. They then selectively incorporate the outcomes of such a development process into their existing operations. This minimises the distraction and likely poor execution that the deployment of the design process internally might otherwise produce. Further, it allows the firm to make a choice eventually from a range of initiatives that fit its strategic priorities and can be realistically integrated into their existing business model.

This approach is also consistent with one of the key precepts of design thinking – that "outsiders" to existing business models or those enmeshed in whatever problem is to be the subject of its attention are least suited to be able to use the process effectively. Further, they are least likely to be able to either identify the problem as a problem or ask the right questions of clients or potential clients in the first place.

References

1. www.duncanhartconsulting.com
2. Both rational and emotional
3. Levitt, T. (1960) "Marketing Myopia", *Harvard Business Review.*
4. Supplemented notoriously, by advertising being utilised to actually create an emotional need in the prospective market for the brand and product in question.
5. See detailed discussion of the importance of building an industry focus and client-based knowledge and insights in both my previous titles *Lean Innovation for Lawyers* and *The Strategic Law Firm*.
6. See by way of example the works of Alex Osterwalder, *Business Model Generation* and *Value Proposition Design* and *The Design Thinking Playbook* by Michael Lewrick.
7. www.ark-group.com/product/lean-innovation-lawyers-creating-and-delivering-innovation-strategy

Milton Keynes UK
Ingram Content Group UK Ltd.
UKHW021914030524
442186UK00023B/361

9 781783 583850